EMAIL ESSENTIALS

HOW TO WRITE EFFECTIVE EMAILS AND BUILD
GREAT RELATIONSHIPS ONE MESSAGE AT A TIME

SHIRLEY TAYLOR

D0168612

Marshall Cavendish
Business

© 2017 Marshall Cavendish International (Asia) Private Limited
Text © Shirley Taylor
Illustrations by Edwin Ng
Cover design by Lorraine Aw

Published in 2017 by Marshall Cavendish Business
An imprint of Marshall Cavendish International
1 New Industrial Road, Singapore 536196

A member of the
Times Publishing Group

Other Marshall Cavendish Offices:
Marshall Cavendish Corporation. 99 White Plains Road, Tarrytown NY 10591–9001, USA • Marshall Cavendish International (Thailand) Co Ltd. 253 Asoke, 12th Flr, Sukhumvit 21 Road, Klongtoey Nua, Wattana, Bangkok 10110, Thailand • Marshall Cavendish (Malaysia) Sdn Bhd, Times Subang, Lot 46, Subang Hi-Tech Industrial Park, Batu Tiga, 40000 Shah Alam, Selangor Darul Ehsan, Malaysia.

Marshall Cavendish is a registered trademark of Times Publishing Limited

National Library Board, Singapore Cataloguing in Publication Data
Name(s): Taylor, Shirley.
Title: Email essentials : how to write effective emails and build great relationships one message at a time / Shirley Taylor.
Description: Singapore : Marshall Cavendish Business, 2017.
Identifier(s): OCN 959914168 | ISBN 978-981-4771-72-6 (paperback)
Subject(s): LCSH: Business writing—Handbooks, manuals, etc. | Electronic mail messages—Handbooks, manuals, etc.
Classification: DDC 808.06665–dc23

Printed in Singapore by Markono Print Media Pte Ltd

CONTENTS

INTRODUCTION

EMAIL IS POSSIBLY one of the greatest inventions of our lifetime. It's having a phenomenal effect on the way we communicate, but that may not always be for the better! Reading, writing and managing email is taking an increasing amount of our time. However, research shows that the major cause of email stress is not its volume but its inappropriate use as a communication tool.

More of us are using email to stay in touch while we are travelling or working from home. We are using desktops and laptops as well as tablets and smart phones. We use email to communicate with friends and family, as well as business clients and colleagues, often all over the globe. People whose jobs never used to involve writing skills are now finding themselves replying to dozens of emails every day.

Most of us comment about the increasing quantity of the messages we receive and the pressure we are under to respond quickly. However, under such pressure, what is happening to the quality of the messages we exchange?

Just as a handshake and eye contact say something about you when you meet someone in person, the approach you take in an email gives an impression as well. Whether you are writing a thank you note, a meeting reminder, a proposal or a sales pitch, what you write and how you write it affects what people think of you, and it affects the image of your organisation.

A well-written message that looks and sounds professional will make it easier for people to want to do business with you. It will help people feel good about communicating with you. It will also help you achieve the right response and get great results.

The fact that you've picked up this book means that you want to make email work more effectively for you. You are interested in using email thoughtfully, presenting yourself and your organisation in a positive light. In this book you will find all the help you need, from managing your mailbox to writing great messages, structuring messages logically, using plain English, touching up your tone, and much more.

You'll also notice some key features that highlight important learning points:

MYTH BUSTER
Here you will find a statement that is not true, with notes on the true facts of the matter.

FAST FACT
Useful snippets of information or special points to remember.

Aha! Moment

This is a 'lightbulb' moment, when we note something you may be able to conclude from a discussion. Don't forget to note your own 'Aha! Moments', perhaps when you receive some extra insight that clarifies an important point.

Try This

Here you'll find a suggestion for how you can put a special point into practice, either at home or at work.

Danger Zone

You'll find some words of warning here, such as things to avoid or precautions to take.

Star Tips

At the end of each chapter you'll find a list of Star Tips — important notes to remind you about the key points.

I hope you'll practise the guidelines I've shared in this book. There are lots of samples in here too, as well as formulas for various scenarios that I know you'll find useful.

Start turning the pages and enjoy the huge rewards it will bring!

Shirley Taylor

ASSESS YOURSELF

What is your current understanding of email?

1. Why shouldn't you type your messages in ALL CAPS?
   a) ALL CAPS implies that you are shouting or yelling.
   b) It causes a strain on the reader's eyes and makes reading more difficult.
   c) It makes you look lazy and uneducated.
   d) All of the above.

2. The most important thing to do with every email message is:
   a) Use spellcheck, write in full sentences and use proper grammar.
   b) Use proper paragraphs and leave a space between paragraphs.
   c) Make sure the email address is correct.
   d) All of the above.

3. You should only forward an email when:
   a) You feel it is important.
   b) You know the other person should have the information.
   c) You include a personal comment about why you are forwarding this message to this specific person.
   d) The topic is commendable and important for other people to read.

4. Which one of these would you say is correct?
   a) It's OK to use big words and long sentences occasionally.
   b) Abbreviations, jargon and buzz words are fine to use in writing.
   c) It's important to use formal, template writing to impress readers.
   d) Passive voice is appropriate for email writing.

5. If you can't reply to a message straight away, what should you do?
   a) Send a brief acknowledgement and say you'll reply as soon as possible.
   b) Carry on with your other work; you'll get round to it later.
   c) Put it in a special 'KIV' or 'Pending' folder.
   d) Delete it.

6. When is it alright to contact people by email about your business?
   a) When you know they really need your service.
   b) Anytime at all — after all, lots of companies do 'cold calling' on the telephone.
   c) Only when they call or email you and ask you for information.
   d) When you know you can save them money.

7. A good way to check the user-friendliness of your message is to:
a) Use lots of abbreviations so the message is short and simple.
b) Run spellcheck because that finds all the errors.
c) Write it all in one paragraph so the message is not too long.
d) Read it out loud with proper tone as if you are speaking to the recipient.

8. A good subject line is:
a) Lengthy, to give as much information as possible.
b) Specific, meaningful, appropriate, relevant and thoughtful.
c) One or two words only.
d) You don't always need to use a subject line.

9. When you are angry about an issue, the best thing to do is:
a) Write an email immediately while it's still at the top of your mind.
b) Draft an email and come back to it after an hour, when you will make changes.
c) Go to the water cooler and tell all your friends about it.
d) Pick up the phone and give the guy a piece of your mind.

10. You can create good rapport with clients by:
a) Always sending email instead of picking up the phone.
b) Using standard, traditional phrases and corporate templates.
c) Using friendly language and a natural style, as if having a conversation.
d) Being very serious and formal in all your emails.

How did you do?

1. The correct answer is (d). ALL CAPS means much more than shouting. Learn more about what's right and what's not in Chapters 1 and 5.

2. Did you answer (d)? All these things are important. See Chapter 1 for a list of common complaints about email in practice.

3. It is always good to know why you are receiving a specific email, so please follow the advice in (c). If you need more help, Chapter 2 is for you.

4. Sorry if you were tricked here, but none of these are correct. It's essential to use plain English today. Find out more in Chapter 6.

5. It's good manners to send a brief acknowledgement, so (a) is the correct answer here. See Chapter 1 for an example.

6. Please don't spam. The correct answer is (c). Learn more about email netiquette in Chapter 3.

7. The golden rule of writing today is to write as if you are speaking, so I do hope you answered (d). Learn more about writing great messages in Chapters 3, 4, 5, 6 and 7.

8. A good subject line is SMART — so the answer is (b). Spruce up your writing skills by referring to Chapter 4.

9. The sensible answer is (b). In email messages, all you have are words, so you must really work on how they will come across to your reader. Touch up your tone in Chapter 8.

10. Yes, (c) is the answer here. You will create a good rapport with everyone if you use a friendly style as if you are having a conversation. Find out more about building great relationships with your readers in Chapter 7.

1

EMAIL – THE PITFALLS AND POTENTIAL

Computers crash, people die, relationships fall apart.
The best we can do is breathe and reboot.
— Carrie Bradshaw, from *Sex and the City*

THE INTERNET IS a place where global information and communication is constantly expanding and evolving. Just as with any culture, there are customs that provide guidelines and cohesiveness to the people involved. That's what this book is all about — helping you understand the rules of the road for email as well as the pitfalls and the potential.

The impact of email on business

Email has had a significant impact on the workplace, and has dramatically changed the way we work. It has certainly helped to reduce the amount of paper correspondence, but on the other hand it has also diminished our face-to-face interactions. For some people, email makes life easier. However, others are feeling the personal disconnection that results from overusing email compared to face-to-face interactions.

Good or bad, email is continuing to impact our daily lives. Let's look at some of the impacts:

1. Email overload

Email overload is a growing problem for most people. Employees are sometimes so overwhelmed with catching up on email that they neglect other critical job duties. Managers are spending so much time reading and replying to emails that they have less time to coach, train and motivate their staff.

FAST FACT

According to research by The Radicati Group, Inc, by the end of 2019 the number of worldwide users of email will exceed 219 million, and over one-third of the worldwide population will be using email. It is expected that over 246 billion emails will be sent per day. And it is estimated that each business email user will be sending and receiving approximately 126 email messages per day.

---

2. Impact on memory

Very often, working with email means you have to develop a good memory. We tend not to print out as many messages as we perhaps should. Also, many companies implement a system in which old messages (say 30 days old) may be deleted automatically from workstations so that the hard disk is not clogged up unnecessarily. Protect yourself by saving paper copies of important messages.

3. Choosing email over telephone

Many people are sending email messages instead of picking up the phone. This is a common complaint when I talk to clients to discuss potential in-house training. On email it may take several back-and-forth messages to reach a satisfactory conclusion when the issue could be resolved in one phone call. Sending emails when a fast response is needed is just not effective. When time is critical, talking with someone in person or making a phone call is much more effective.

4. Virtual teams

Email has enabled companies to have more diverse work teams, spread out over different locations, often in different countries. Team members can interact and collaborate without needing face-to-face contact. These teams are using software so they share files and hold virtual meetings. But of course email also goes back and forth.

5. Less personalisation

A big drawback of the huge growth in email has been less use of more personalised communication. Employees may overuse email for contacting prospective clients where telephone contact would be much more instant. Work colleagues often prefer to sit at their desks and send emails rather than walking across the office to interact personally with team members. Personal interaction would enable immediate feedback, both verbally and non-verbally. This just isn't possible with email. Overuse of email is very often not helping to build rapport and develop relationships with people. Therefore, the effectiveness of this communication is often reduced.

 DANGER ZONE
Email may be a very powerful form of communication, but it can also result in people feeling very disconnected.

6. Misinterpretation

It's very difficult to convey tone in an email, so a reader may not read something in the way you thought you wrote it. This could lead to misunderstanding or conflict. It's so much easier to express the real meaning behind your message when you're looking someone in the eye. Even on the phone you can hear tone of voice and feel emotions. Email can make it too easy to avoid face-to-face discussions and send messages that lack any feeling. So despite the benefits of email, it can lead to feeling disconnected, often making the workplace feel cold and impersonal.

7. No real guidelines

As there have been no real guidelines laid down on how to work with email or how to write email messages, some frustrations are inevitable. A major problem for some people is simply being unable to adjust their communication styles to this new medium. When email is used effectively it can be very powerful indeed. However, when it is used ineffectively it can be costly, annoying and damaging to a company's reputation.

MYTH BUSTER

We don't need training in how to use email. We can pick it up with experience.

Wrong! Many organisations provide a wide range of training for employees — from supervisory training to communication skills, from leadership skills to powerful presentations. In view of the increasing impact that communication has on business, I'm glad to see that many companies are providing training in effective business writing, not only for business letters and reports, but also for email.

Why do we love email?

In terms of the time factor alone, it's easy to see why email is the preferred choice for written communication. Let's take a look at some more reasons why we love email:

- It's written. You can edit and check it before you send it. The recipient can read it, forward it to someone else, perhaps print it out and file it away.

- It's time-zone friendly. Email is great for international communication over different time zones.

- It's quick. Messages are usually delivered in seconds. They may not be read so quickly, but they will be in the recipient's inbox.

- It's cheap. Of course you need to buy a computer and a modem, and (sometimes) pay an Internet service provider. But no matter where your recipient is, each message should cost very little.

- It's flexible. You can forward or send multiple copies of messages easily, and attach documents to messages without any hassle.

- You can attach files. As long as your recipient has the software to open it, you can attach a spreadsheet, a report, photographs, a game, a video — virtually anything!

- It's non-intrusive. You decide when to read your mail and when to reply.

- It can be prioritised. When you open your email first thing in the morning you can prioritise your email-related work for the day. Simple or urgent tasks can be dealt with quickly before getting involved in more heavy-duty or non-urgent work.

- You see the history of each communication. This is a great tool so you can scroll down and remind yourself about previous discussions on the topic.

DANGER ZONE

Avoid the temptation of keeping your email alert switched on the whole time. If you are working on an important report or spreadsheet, you need to focus. You can't concentrate if your pop-up keeps popping up every few minutes, or if that 'ding' keeps 'dinging'! Be sensible and switch off your email alert when you need to focus.

Why don't we love email?

I did a survey asking people about problems they are experiencing with email. Here is a summary of what I discovered:

1. Constant interruptions to your working day

Most email programs have an instant messaging facility that means you are interrupted regularly by an alert like a little buzz or a ping. These interruptions can interfere with your planned work and add frustration and stress to your day. In some companies, however, staff say they must leave their alert on all the time because their boss insists, just in case something urgent is missed. Unless it's a specific requirement of your job, I strongly suggest that you consider switching off your email alert — you will be able to focus on your report or your spreadsheet, and you will feel a greater sense of achievement by doing so. Then when you need a break from your project, you can go back to your email and give it your full attention.

2. It wastes time

Composing and replying to emails can sometimes take up a lot of time that could be better spent on your real job. However, it is common courtesy to reply to email as soon as possible, even if it's just an acknowledgement saying you will give the matter more attention and get back to the writer later:

> Hi Janet
>
> Thanks for your message. Can you please give me a few days to look into this, and I'll get back to you by Thursday.
>
> Many thanks
>
> Wendy

I like this advice from one of my workshop participants, who told me that he tries never to click on an email message more than twice. He said, 'I always try to respond as soon as I've read a message, or delete it. If I'm pushed for time, I scan all my messages and then answer the urgent ones straight away. I deal with the others whenever I have a free moment.'

3. It's not always the best choice of medium

It can sometimes take the exchange of many email messages to resolve a situation or a problem that could have been dealt with swiftly and efficiently by a telephone call or face-to-face discussion. Before you send an email message, ask yourself if it really is the best way to deliver the message. It may be convenient and quick, but it would not be suitable, for example, for passing on bad news or dealing with an uncomfortable situation. In such cases, a call or a discussion in person may be much better.

Oh, hi Martin, I was just going to send you an email. It's so much nicer to hear your voice though.

Aha! Moment

Handling a delicate or sensitive situation is better done by the human voice, either in person or on the phone, as it can convey sympathy and/or other emotions.

4. Confidentiality can be a problem

Keeping something confidential is almost impossible with email. Your employer may have the right to read, without your consent or knowledge, any email messages you send or receive at work. Therefore, be careful what you write, in case it comes back to haunt you!

5. Email overload

The traffic problem seems to be one of the main issues with email. Some managers receive hundreds of messages every day, so ways to deal with this overload must be developed. It's too easy to forward messages on to lots of people, 'just in case', whether or not they really need to see them. This can cause extreme annoyance as well as overloading networks, not to mention being a complete waste of people's time.

FAST FACT

Many organisations issue instructions to their employees to keep individual mailbox size down. Once a mailbox exceeds that limit, employees are unable to send out or receive messages. This forces staff to keep their mailboxes to a manageable size, and enforces good housekeeping habits. This system works very well in most organisations and is also cost-effective.

6. Overflowing inboxes

Email messages that are not deleted are causing not a paper mountain but an electronic mountain, so you must do your filing regularly. Make some time to go through messages and delete those you no longer need. And if you receive copies of email messages that you don't really need to see, tell the sender so that it doesn't happen again:

> Hi John
>
> You have been copying me in on this correspondence for some time, but I really don't need to receive them. Please don't include me in the cc list of these and similar messages in future.
>
> Many thanks
>
> Lay Hong

7. Increased stress levels

It's official. Research shows that one of the top 10 causes of workplace stress is the pressure of keeping up with email messages. This ranks higher than having a bad relationship with your boss and dealing with customer complaints! It's a real problem. Let experience point the way to letting email work for you, instead of against you.

8. More haste, less speed

Many people feel that because it's email, it has to be acted on instantly. This is adding to the pressures that people already face. Not only this, but because email is seen as urgent, some writers don't take much care with spelling, punctuation, grammar or structure. So what's happening is that rushed messages become garbled, with spelling, grammar and punctuation errors, poor structure, and with no real focus. The end result is that such messages are not effective and lead to that inevitable 'ding-dong' of further emails to clarify!

9. Junk email or spam

Some people are using email to send unsolicited advertising, called 'junk email' or 'spam'. Modern anti-spam filters block more than 99 per cent of junk messages, but spam is still a big business. Unsolicited junk mail accounts for 86 per cent of the world's email traffic, with about 400 billion spam messages sent every day, according to Talos, a digital threat research division of Cisco Systems.

10. Death of conversation

People who used to speak to each other regularly are nowadays communicating via email. Sometimes when my phone rings and it's a person I usually communicate with on email, I say, 'Oh hello, a real voice! How wonderful to *talk* to you!' So please, pick up the telephone now and again — it's great to talk!

Aha! Moment

Email is a 'double-edged sword'. There are many things to love about email, but there are many things we need to be very cautious and careful about. It's important to learn to use email well.

Email enhances efficiency

It's important to continually keep up with the technology that makes it easier to stay in touch with customers and colleagues. But email should not be taken for granted. This fabulous technology should be looked upon as a tool to enhance communication rather than a replacement for communication. Email is a wonderful tool that makes it possible for us to achieve more, with greater efficiency and professionalism. Remember, though, that email is only a supplement and should never replace human interaction.

Let's look at just a few other ways in which email is helping us to increase our efficiency:

- **Connection to people and information:** Email helps you to stay informed and keeps other people informed more effectively than would be possible if we didn't have it.

- **Improved project management:** With such a global community these days, working together on a project can prove to be quite difficult when people are in different companies, places and time zones. Email makes this process so much easier.

- **Team building:** Email is helping to make group work more effective. All team members must be briefed with a common set of objectives so that they realise the importance of replying promptly to all team mail. They also need compatible software so that they can attach and read all the documents that will be distributed to members.

- **Global communication:** With Internet connections, it's possible to reach out way beyond the boundaries of your organisation. You can join discussion groups and mailing lists relating to your specific interests, and subsequently engage in discussions with thousands of people around the world.

- **Better record management:** With email now often replacing telephone conversations, letters and memos, much of the information is in one place, so it becomes easier to manage. All messages regarding a specific topic can be kept in a special folder. Alternatively a search will quickly call up all the messages that meet certain criteria.

- **Virtual meetings:** Before email came about, many more meetings took place. It is sometimes quite difficult to get lots of people together at the same venue and time, and with pressures of work, it could be a week or more before everyone involved could get together. Email solves this problem. A message can be sent to everyone involved, the issue or problem can be discussed with everyone being copied, and a lot of time can be saved.

- **Collaborative work:** Email makes it easy and cheap to share photographs, graphics, files, even video. Whether your colleague is in the next office or at the other side of the world, distance is no longer an issue. As long as everyone has compatible versions of the necessary software, it's easy to attach anything to an email message.

 AHA! MOMENT
While it's important to keep up-to-date with technology, this shouldn't be taken to the extent that we avoid talking to our customers and colleagues personally. Email is a supplement to, not a replacement for, interaction. It's a useful tool that helps us to create more time and more opportunities for everyone in the organisation to do even better.

Handheld electronic devices

Email doesn't only come to our desks. Many of us now carry email around with us on our mobile phones. This often results in being on call 24 hours a day, every day, even on weekends. Apart from never being free from the demands of work, this also leads to another problem: messages typed with our thumbs often contain errors and can end up becoming quite terse. You might include a tagline such as 'Sent from my iPhone', thinking that your recipient may be more forgiving of mistakes or brusqueness. However, I'm not convinced that this will always work.

A friend recently told me that he now does 75 per cent of his emailing through his mobile phone and that he has to adapt his language for this new medium. Things he would not normally do on his computer, such as abbreviating words or not starting off with a greeting, he is actually doing on his electronic device.

Consider this message that he may have sent if he'd been sitting at his computer:

Hi John

Great to hear from you. I'm glad you can come down to Singapore next week to discuss this exciting project. If you can let me have your proposal within the next couple of days, I can discuss it with our management and send you any urgent questions before we meet.

Look forward to seeing you.

Michael

If sending this same message from his electronic device, the message would become:

> Pls send yr proposal so I can put to mgmt and send you any q's. Tnks.
>
> (Sent from my iPhone)

You can see what I mean about the message becoming terse, not to mention abbreviated. It could actually ruin the personal rapport that he may have built up with this recipient. Such abbreviated messages may also lead to more back-and-forth emailing for clarification, which would not be necessary if he had either picked up the phone or waited till he could give the message a more considered response.

Another concern is the tendency to become addicted to checking our handhelds constantly. Imagine you are downtown on your way to an appointment and you bump into a client. While you're standing on the street having a discussion with her, she sneaks a peek at her electronic device. How would you feel about that? Not impressed, right? Never underestimate the importance of body language, especially in making eye contact — and that means with the other person, not with your mobile phone!

It's worse if you check your email on your electronic device in formal meetings, or sneakily try to send a text message imagining that no one will notice. Everyone notices!

⚠️ **DANGER ZONE**
Etiquette applies to handhelds too. Avoid checking your handheld during dinner, at a movie or concert, in a meeting, in the playground with your children, or when out on a date!

What goes wrong in written communication?

I'm sure we must all have received written communication that failed to achieve its objectives. Whether it's email, letters, memos or faxes, have you ever received any communication that failed in these areas?

- Your gender is changed to Mr instead of Mrs or Miss.

- The purpose of the message is not clearly stated.

- The response required is not clearly stated.

- The message is all jumbled up with no thought given to structure.

- The writer uses long sentences and long paragraphs that look uninviting.

- The message is full of long-winded jargon and redundancies.

- The tone is wrong — critical, patronising or intimidating.

- Vital details are missing, so you have to send another message to clarify.

Why do these problems happen? One reason is that, as a sender, you are not there physically to help to put your message across with body language, gestures, facial expressions, tone of voice and your personality. Some other reasons are:

- It takes time to write and to reply. Some messages need more thought than others to work out exactly what you want or need to say.

- You may be trying to think up too many words that will look impressive.

- If your thinking is muddled, the structure of your message will be muddled too.

- If you are thinking as you write, sometimes you will waffle and your writing can become unclear and confusing.

All these problems can be improved with experience, with constant awareness, and by taking a sincere interest in the way you write.

Turning problems into potential

So now we all have a good understanding of the problems that can happen with email. We also know how to turn them all around to make use of the full potential of this wonderful communication medium. Here are some suggestions:

1. Remember you are talking to a human being

When you are holding a conversation online (and in effect that's what an email exchange is) it's easy for your correspondent to misinterpret your meaning, and vice versa. You can't use facial expressions, gestures or tone of voice to communicate your meanings as you can in a real conversation. Written words are all you have, so make the most of them. Put yourself in the other person's place and imagine how you would feel on receiving that message. While it's good to stand up for yourself, it is important to try not to hurt other people's feelings.

The key here is to think before you click that 'Send' button. Ask yourself, 'Would I say this to the person's face?' If not, then you must edit, rewrite and reread. Don't send your message until you are quite sure that you would feel just as comfortable saying the words to the person face-to-face.

2. Make your message clear and to the point

In Chapters 4 and 5, we'll look in detail at how to compose effective email messages. The main rule to remember is to make sure your messages are clear and logical. Long words in lengthy sentences will not impress — they will confuse. So pay attention to the content of your writing as well as to the structure and flow of your message.

In email we are all judged by one thing alone — the quality of our writing. Learn to love the written word, learn to play with the written word, learn to make the most of the written word. And please: use initial capitals just as you would in a traditional letter, and avoid using hard-to-understand abbreviations, which will only confuse and annoy your reader.

A friend told me that she received a professional enquiry that was written in very, very casual, almost instant-messenger-like language. This made my friend feel that the sender was not so proficient or respectful, and probably less educated. My friend then called her to discuss the matter rather than email a response, and during their conversation she found the lady to be very pleasant and friendly. My friend decided to tell her the different impression she'd received from her email, and the lady was horrified and very glad of the opportunity to do something about it. Ever since then, her subsequent emails have been clear and concise, and very effective indeed.

3. Make your message look good

I know part of the beauty of email is its speed, but how long does it take to write 'Dear Tom' or finish off by writing your name? How long does it take to start a new paragraph every few lines? How long does it take to put a blank line between those paragraphs? Get into these good habits from now on. Looking good online (format and structure) goes hand in hand with sounding good (composition and tone), and these give your reader a good impression of you.

4. Respect your reader's time

Research shows that we all have more work to do and less time to do it. The number of email messages in a person's inbox only adds to this already weighty workload. So show some respect for your reader by keeping your messages brief and concise, including all the relevant details, structuring them logically, using an appropriate salutation and close, and including a clear and specific subject line.

5. Think twice before you hit 'Send'

Before sending any message, think twice before you hit 'Send'. I always suggest to my training participants that they need to take off their own head and put on the head of the reader. Read it through carefully, as if you were the reader, and ask yourself:

- Is it easy to read?

- Is my meaning quite clear?

- Is the content hurtful or offensive?

- Is the tone appropriate?

- Is the action stated clearly?

- Is the message right for email? Or would a letter, phone call or face-to-face discussion be better?

International considerations

In my workshops I'm often asked what it means when someone begins an email with 'I hope this email finds you well'. This seems to be a very misunderstood greeting, but it simply means 'I hope you are fine today'.

This emphasises the importance of using appropriate language when emailing people from another country, or whose mother tongue may not be English. Be cautious about overusing idiomatic phrases that everyone around you understands but may be difficult to understand by someone not absolutely fluent in your language.

In general, when emailing people whose mother tongue is not English, it is best to use short, simple sentences that will be much easier to understand. Keep your messages as short as possible without letting meaning suffer and use simple words instead of long ones. Niceties are acceptable, to a point, but please don't overdo it. Learn more about simplifying your language in Chapter 5.

When crossing international boundaries with your emails, it's better to be a little more cautious and use a slightly more formal tone for your messages at first. It will then be easy to progress from formal to friendly as you get to know your recipient better. It would weaken your position if you had to step backwards from friendly to formal.

STAR TIPS
for making the most of email

1. Adapt your communication style to make email work for you, not against you.

2. Use email appropriately to enhance your reputation and your organisation's image.

3. Switch off your email alert when you need to concentrate or focus on an important project.

4. Consider if a quick word with a colleague or a simple phone call to a client could resolve an issue more efficiently than using email.

5. Enhance relationships with colleagues and clients by using email effectively.

6. Pay attention to the tone, language and structure of your emails, as all these impact your reader.

7. Don't let email be a replacement for communication. It is a tool for enhancing communication.

8. When emailing across cultures, keep your language simple and your sentences short.

9. Avoid constantly checking email on your handheld. It will make you seem rude and antisocial.

10. Be cautious when using colloquial phrases in email — your reader may not understand them.

2

MANAGING
YOUR MAILBOX

*Men are only as good as their technical development
allows them to be.*
— George Orwell

SOME PEOPLE FIND the volume of mail in their inbox quite overwhelming. Are you a slave to that little beep or ping that comes from your computer, sometimes every few seconds? Has that little noise programmed you so that every time you hear it, you immediately dive back into your email to see what's there?

There seems to be a compulsion to keep checking our email, and this is not just a real draining effect on your time, it's also taking you away from your other work.

Never fear, help is at hand. All it takes is a little attention to detail and some time management skills. You can regain your power and get some balance back into your working life if you resolve to put email in its place as a tool that can help you, not control you. In this chapter, we will discuss tips and techniques to help you to organise your mail, your mailbox and your time.

If email hasn't yet become such an overwhelming burden in your life, beware — it can happen almost overnight! So don't wait until breaking point to implement these time-saving techniques. Start now!

Seven deadly sins of email management

Read this list of seven deadly sins of email management and tick the ones that apply to you. If you tick a few of these items, you need help. This chapter is just what you need.

- ☐ You deal with work in fragments, jumping from one project to another, from one message to another, without any clear organisation.

- ☐ You click on each message and read it more than once, sometimes several times, before responding.

- ☐ You take on work that should be dealt with by other people instead of forwarding it when appropriate.

- ☐ You keep too many messages in your mailbox without action, so your inbox gets longer and longer.

- ☐ You don't answer messages completely, so recipients end up having to come back for clarification.

- ☐ You don't use all the functions of your mailer such as address book, templates and automatic signature.

- ☐ You spend too long every day writing email messages.

'You've got mail' flow chart

This flow chart shows all the basic steps you must go through when you receive mail:

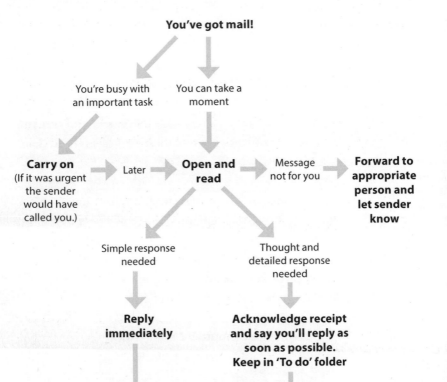

Receiving mail

'You've got mail!' Your email alert can be received with a smile or a snarl depending on what sort of day you are having. Some people have their message alert on all the time, so every time they receive a message they are interrupted by a little beep, a flag, a horn, a voice, or even the national anthem!

Here's my suggestion: when you are working on an important project, consider switching off your email alert so that you can work uninterrupted. These constant interruptions prevent you from focusing properly on your 'real work'. Surely nothing can be so important that it can't wait for an hour or two?

A friend of mine has the best idea. She said, 'When I need to concentrate on an important report, I just can't have the alert beeping or popping up all the time, otherwise I wouldn't be able to focus, so I switch off the alert temporarily. I get my report finished quicker and it's more likely to be well-written. Then when I've finished, I can concentrate on replying to emails to the same effect.'

Processing mail

When you are going through your messages, scan each one carefully. Read the subject line and the first paragraph. If necessary scan a little further into the message. Then make a decision whether you will do one of these four things:

1. Save or print it for reading later
2. Delete it
3. Forward it to someone else
4. Act on it

If you leave a message in your inbox with no evaluation at all, it simply means that you will go back to read it again and again. This is just the same as moving pieces of paper around your desk from one tray to another — it is a total waste of time.

When receiving lots of email daily, it's imperative that you quickly read through them all before replying to any, especially when the same exchange involves many different people. An immediate response to an earlier email message may not be the most efficient response based on what may have been mentioned in another message. You can certainly save time and avoid the need for an embarrassed 'Sorry, you're right, I hadn't read that yet' response.

DANGER ZONE

Don't for one minute think you can just keep your received messages in your inbox and your sent messages in your 'Sent' folder. Imagine if you were to put all your paper mail into one in-tray without any sorting. You would quickly reach a point where you cannot find anything at all. Instead, you keep a number of files, each one labelled, so it is easy to file and to find paper mail. The same principle applies to email.

1. Save for later

Messages that you save may be:

- Lower priority

- Messages that don't need immediate attention

- For reading only

Make sure you file these messages somewhere so you can find them later. Don't leave them in your inbox to be moved around and revisited several times. You may decide to print a message out or put it in a 'Read later' folder to look at later (on the train or at home or while waiting for an appointment).

2. Delete it

Unfortunately, we all receive irrelevant messages or junk email (spam), just like we receive junk mail through the post. It's a fact of life. Since you usually throw paper junk mail straight into the wastepaper bin, that's what you do with junk email too. Don't waste any time thinking or worrying about it — just delete it. You can often recognise spam as soon as you see the subject line or the sender's address.

Your email program will have a junk mail folder too, so do make sure you check it regularly, just in case some legitimate mail lands in there. You may also be able to tag an email as spam so that anything else from the same address will automatically go into your junk folder.

Fast Fact

Don't even bother opening email with subject lines like these:

- Want to Earn Easy $????
- Earn $$$ while you SLEEP!
- Make 1000% on every Sale!

These messages are spam and should be deleted straight away.

3. Forward it to someone else

If you are not the right person to handle a particular message, then forward it to someone else. However, do remember that it's good manners to include a note about why you are sending a particular message. Don't just forward a message without a note. Simply click on 'Forward' and add a few lines — perhaps, 'I think this is your department. Can I pass it over to you?' Also, it's very important to let the sender know where you have forwarded their message and the address of the person they should contact in future.

4. Act on it

Many messages require a simple, straightforward response. If you reply immediately, it's done with and you can forget about it. If you need to give the matter some thought, or do some research first, then put the message in your 'Drafts' folder or highlight the message with the 'Priority' setting, or whatever feature is available on your mailer. It is courteous, however, to send a quick reply first to acknowledge the message and inform the writer that you will get back to them soon. For example:

> Hi John
>
> Thanks for your message. I need to check up on a few things before I can reply, so please give me a couple of days and I'll get back to you as soon as I can.
>
> Mark

You may need to add this to your written 'Action' list that you keep on your desk (or on your computer) so that you prioritise the issue. When you have all the information necessary to reply to the email, give it the consideration it deserves and reply fully to each point.

MYTH BUSTER

You feel you need to reply to every email message.
False. Just like real conversations, email exchanges have natural endings too. If there's no real reason to reply, then don't!

Fast Fact

Having a discussion by email is called a 'thread'. Remember to keep the original subject line throughout the email conversation as this helps people to keep track of the thread. Your mailer should allow you to keep all messages with the same subject line together, so it is easy to keep track.

Auto-reply messages

If you are going to be away from the office for any length of time, especially on vacation or public holidays, activate your auto-reply message. In this way all incoming messages will receive an automatic reply and people will not be kept in the dark, wondering why you have not replied. Similarly, auto-responding software enables you to redirect certain messages to other people to handle. This is generally used in larger organisations.

> Subject: Auto-reply: Away from office
>
> Thanks for your message. I'm away from the office on a short vacation from 24 to 28 July. For urgent matters, please contact Rekha at rekha@sttstraining.com or telephone 9123 9199. Otherwise I will respond to you when I return to the office on 29 July.
>
> Many thanks
>
> Shirley

DANGER ZONE
Please avoid this common mistake seen in many auto-responders: 'I'm away on course.' A ship may be 'on course'. But you are 'on a course'!

Using folders

Given the quantity of emails arriving in your inbox, you will find it useful to create a system of folders in which to file and save the messages you want to keep. You may find it useful to replicate the system of folders you use on your computer when you do this. For example, I use Outlook for Mac, so in my inbox there are individual folders for each of my key work clients, plus I also have additional folders named 'Home', 'Lawyer', 'Accountant', etc. I regularly transfer messages to these respective folders, at least once or twice a week. This ensures the folders are always up-to-date when I need to refer to them.

Using filters (or rules)

It's easy for your inbox to become inundated with incoming mail, especially if you subscribe to automated mailing lists. When you have so much in your inbox it becomes easy to miss the really important messages. Filters help you to deal with this problem. They are sets of rules in your mailer program that you set up so that your mail is sorted into different piles, usually according to the sender and the subject matter. Messages are then filed automatically into the different folders. Some filters will highlight key messages on the incoming mail list with priority codes or colours.

You can easily create a simple filing system by organising your incoming mail into folders — this saves you valuable searching time. Examples of folders include 'Work', 'Personal', 'Ezines', 'Articles', 'To Do'. You can also use your email program like a personal organiser, storing draft messages and reminders in your Monday through Sunday or 'To Do' folders.

Your filtering system can be set up to:

- Place messages from mailing lists into appropriate folders so that clutter is removed from your inbox.

- Delete unwanted messages.

- Reply to messages with a courteous standard response so that correspondents know action is underway.

- Detect messages that need special priority so that they sit at the top of your list.

The benefits of being organised

Just like a successful paper management system is a key element in organisational and time management skills, a good filing system is also the key to successful email management. With a good filing system you will be able to file messages quickly and find them again easily.

Questions to ask yourself about your current filing system are:

- Is your inbox full of messages that are read but not filed?

- Do you have difficulty deciding where to file certain messages?

- Do you have difficulty finding messages again after you have filed them?

- Do you have difficulty identifying messages where action is outstanding?

- Are some folders bulging with mixed topics that should really be broken up into sub-folders?

- Are your folders and sub-folders clearly labelled and easy to access?

- Is the filing system practical and easy to use?

Subject-based filing systems are most popular with email. You must decide which subjects suit your work, as well as whether sub-categories will be useful within folders. You may also want to create other folders for things like Action, Awaiting Reply, Drafts, etc. Folders will usually be displayed on-screen in alphabetical order. If you want to get something to the top of your list, start it with 'AAA' or consider making them sub-folders of a folder called 'Active'. When something is no longer active, move it out of this folder into its own named folder. Similarly, anything that you don't need to look at very often (perhaps even personal email if allowed by your company) can be placed at the bottom of the list by starting the folder name with 'ZZZ'.

Once you have considered all these factors you will be able to create a mail management system that is much more user-friendly. It may take a few hours to revamp your filing system, especially if radical changes are necessary, but you will see the benefits straight away, with immediate saving in time and frustration.

TRY THIS
Go on! Sort out the folders in your email program now. You know it makes sense.

When not to use email

Good email management also means knowing when you should not use email, and realising that in some situations you need to take great care in composing your message.

1. When messages are confidential
Email messages can sometimes be read by other people, certainly by the system administrator if there is one at your organisation. There is also the problem that your recipient could easily forward your message to someone else, perhaps inappropriately. If the information you want to send is very confidential, it would be better to put it in a letter or a memo in an envelope marked as confidential. Alternatively,

send it as a fax but only if you know the recipient will be at the other end waiting to receive it.

2. When messages are long and complicated

Email recipients want to process messages quickly, and they usually read messages on-screen. Long, complicated messages do not look good on email. If you really must include a lot of information in an email message, make sure you structure it such that the reader can scan it quickly for essential detail and then study it further when it is more convenient. See my Four-Point Plan for structuring email messages in Chapter 9.

3. When there are many issues to resolve or clarify

With email there can sometimes be quite a lot of to-ing and fro-ing when an issue has lots of questions to be answered. This can result in lengthy and often frustrating email conversations. Sometimes it is easier and saves time for everyone if you pick up the telephone to ask questions and receive immediate replies.

4. When messages are indiscreet

When you send an email message ask yourself if you would want the message posted on the company notice board, because that's really what could happen. Email can easily be copied, printed or forwarded. Please don't ever use email to bad-mouth a colleague or employer, to conduct a romantic affair, to pass on gossip, or to discuss office politics. The potential for embarrassment is huge, not to mention the possibility of finding yourself out of a job.

5. When you are angry

When angry words are written, they can be read and reread over and over again as well as forwarded to others and used against you. If you have something unpleasant to discuss with someone, pick up the telephone or discuss it face-to-face. Never use email if you are angry, or your words could come back to haunt you.

MYTH BUSTER

If I send an incriminating, abusive message, I always delete it immediately from my workstation, so no one can find out about it anyway.

Wrong! Your messages could still be hanging around in cyberspace somewhere. Your IT colleagues are most probably backing up your company's servers, so anything you say can always come back to haunt you when you least expect it!

6. When the message is emotive or sensitive

With the written word there is no body language, intonation or gestures that could help in figuring out the meaning. As such it can be easily misinterpreted and you could quite innocently cause offence to your reader. If the topic is emotive or sensitive, or if your words could be misinterpreted, then don't put it in writing. Such matters are much better dealt with face-to-face so that gestures and tone of voice come into play and your words can be softened as appropriate.

It's always best to put yourself in the other person's position when deciding on the best way to send a message. How will they feel when they read your message? Will your purpose and intent come across clearly, or are misunderstandings possible?

STAR TIPS
for effective email management

1. Consider turning off your message alert so you can really focus when working on important projects that require concentration.

2. Organise your mail into folders with email, just as you do with paper files.

3. Set up a filter system so that incoming mail is automatically placed in the appropriate folders for ease of reference.

4. Clear your clutter regularly; this applies to old messages too. Know when to hit 'Delete'.

5. Set up a filing system that is practical for you, using folders and sub-folders. Revamp your filing system regularly to make it as user-friendly as possible.

6. Check your 'Sent' messages folder regularly and delete old messages that you do not need to keep.

7. Change your auto-reply every time you use it, to keep the content relevant and current.

8. Keep copies of important messages and consider archiving messages that you may need later.

9. Make a decision with every email: save, delete, forward or act on it.

10. Start implementing time-saving techniques.

Save - Delete
FWD - Act on it

3

NURTURING YOUR EMAIL NETIQUETTE

Netiquette: rules about the proper and polite way to communicate with other people when you are using the Internet.
— Merriam Webster

ETIQUETTE MEANS the rules of good manners and behaviour, so 'netiquette' has become a set of rules for behaving appropriately online — network etiquette.

Cyberspace has its own culture, and whenever we enter a new culture it's bound to happen that we commit a few blunders. You may be misunderstood. You may offend people. You may take offence where none was intended. In cyberspace it's also easy to forget that you are interacting with real live human beings.

For all these reasons, many people make all kinds of mistakes when communicating online.

In this chapter, I hope to clear up some key rules of the road for netiquette, and offer some general guidelines for behaviour in cyberspace. We will also look at some further aspects of writing email messages, and yes we are even looking at the basics of punctuation. I make no apologies for this because if you can't get full stops and commas in the right place, then you could confuse readers. It's as simple as that. Many people haven't done any kind of refresher for this type of thing since schooldays, so I hope you will be glad of an opportunity to brush up your cyber-grammar skills!

I have also included some 'just for fun' items — emoticons and abbreviations. They should not really be used in business email, but I have included them here for those of you who want to use them in personal messages.

Seven deadly sins of email netiquette

Read this list of seven deadly sins of email netiquette and tick the ones that apply to you. If you tick a few of these items, you'll need to read this chapter carefully.

- ☐ You often send abb msgs to pple u know well. LOL.

- ☐ You write your email messages sloppily because you don't consider it important for an email message to be as perfect as a business letter.

- ☐ You don't run spellcheck before you send a message, even though it's full of spelling errors.

- ☐ Your email is often misunderstood because you never bother with your grammar and you often use the wrong words.

- ☐ You include emoticons in all your messages, whether personal or business. :)

- ☐ You never include an opening greeting or a closing in your email messages.

- ☐ You often let your emotions get the better of you by writing angry or rude messages that upset your readers.

First impressions are important

Whether we like to admit it or not, we often judge people on first impressions, and vice versa. People look at the colour of our skin, our eyes, hair, our clothes, our age, even our weight. With email this is not possible, but you will be judged by the quality of your writing. Spelling and grammar are important! So if you spend a lot of time on email (and who doesn't?) it's worth brushing up on these important basics.

I hope I will be forgiven by those of you who are fully conversant with the rules of good writing, punctuation and grammar. This may not be a section that you will need to refer to often. However, many people are unsure of precisely where an apostrophe should go, when to use a full stop instead of a comma, how to put together a grammatically correct sentence, and so on. This section should help you by clarifying all the basics of the English language, punctuation and grammar.

Basic grammar

I don't want to go into nouns, adverbs, pronouns, etc. Let's keep it really simple here. A sentence contains a subject and a verb, and expresses a complete thought.

subject   verb
This <u>new book</u> on email writing skills <u>is</u> on sale in all bookstores.

subject   verb
A <u>registration form</u> to attend all these seminars <u>was</u> enclosed with the letter.

subject (plural)   verb (plural)
<u>Good manners</u> when writing a business email <u>are</u> very important.

subject (plural)   verb (plural)
The <u>tools</u> built into your PowerPoint program <u>make</u> it easy to create a presentation.

FAST FACT

You will avoid subject-verb agreement errors if you keep your sentences short and simple.

Punctuation made simple

When you speak, the listener is helped by the intonation in your voice, pauses, emphasis, as well as body language. When you write, punctuation carries out all the same functions. Punctuation helps the reader to make sense of your writing.

Commas

Commas provide pauses in sentences, and they help to manage the flow of thought. Commas are used:

- When two or more items are listed:

    I really love chocolate, cupcakes and cookies.

    I need to buy paper, pens, envelopes and a notebook.

    Many people prefer to use a serial comma (also known as an Oxford comma), where a comma is placed before the word 'and', like this:

    My favourite sandwiches are chicken, bacon, and cheese and pickle.

    Using the serial comma here does make the meaning clearer. It's very clear that the writer is listing three types of sandwiches: one is chicken, one is bacon, and the last one is cheese and pickle.

- To follow an introductory dependent clause, or to show where there would be a short natural pause if you were speaking:

    This candidate has the relevant qualifications, but the other one has more experience.

    As soon as we obtain additional revenue, we can buy new stock.

- To show where something has been added, like names, designations or other explanatory details:

    I will ask our Customer Service Manager, Robert Chan, to call you.

> Fauziah Suki, my assistant, will be in touch with you soon about this.

> Please switch off all electronic devices, including mobile phones, during the flight.

- In a sentence where two complete thoughts are separated by 'but', 'or', 'yet', 'so', 'for', 'and' or 'nor':

> I believe this candidate has the relevant qualifications, but he does not have appropriate past experience.

Here, the first complete thought is: I believe this candidate has the relevant qualifications. The second complete thought is: he does not have appropriate past experience. We put a comma immediately after the first complete thought. Try reading this out, and you will see that you need a pause here.

> Mr Lim is in a meeting right now with James, and Sarah is not back from vacation until next Monday.

In this sentence, if we didn't have the comma after 'James', the reader would be very confused. You try it as though the comma were missing, and you'll see how useful it is to place a comma here.

Colons
Colons are used:

- To introduce a list:

> Many items are on sale today: telephones, computers, printers, fax machines.

- To join two clearly related ideas:

  My website gives more details of my speaking and training:
  www.shirleytaylor.com

Semi-colons

Semi-colons are most commonly used to represent a pause longer than a comma but shorter than a full stop. Here are some examples of their use:

  We must buy the new book for all staff; it will be useful for reference.

  These questions don't require answers; they are just intended to make you think.

To be honest, I have stopped using semi-colons in my writing. I don't even like to confuse my workshop participants with them. I think we can manage fine by putting full stops here instead of semi-colons (but not commas).

Apostrophes

Apostrophes seem to cause the most confusion, but they really aren't as difficult as they may seem. An apostrophe is used:

- To indicate omission of a letter or letters:

  When <u>you're</u> writing email, <u>it's</u> important that you <u>don't</u> forget the rules of good writing.

  you are it is do not

- To show ownership or possession:

Singular	Plural
the customer's problem	the customers' problems
the woman's shoes	the women's shoes
the man's tie	the men's ties
the director's car	the directors' cars
the manager's chair	the managers' chairs

 FAST FACT

Remember that 'it's' should only be used when you mean 'it is' or 'it has':

<u>It's</u> been a lot of fun watching the puppy chasing <u>its</u> tail.
It has   Don't use the apostrophe here

Common mistakes with commas

One of the most common mistakes I see every day in emails I receive is when writers put commas in the wrong place, where there should be a full stop instead:

- ✗ It was good to see you last week, thanks for the great lunch.
- ✓ **It was good to see you last week. Thanks for the great lunch.**

- ✗ I shall be in Seoul next month, however, my schedule is quite tight.
- ✓ **I shall be in Seoul next month. However, my schedule is quite tight.**

✗ I need this report by Tuesday, please let me know if this is possible.

✓ **I need this report by Tuesday. Please let me know if this is possible.**

Many people tell me, 'Oh but Shirley, the second part relates to the first part of the sentence, so that's why I've put a comma.' I can understand this reasoning, but the bottom line is that in all these examples we have two complete thoughts. A good rule is to say sentences out loud so you can really tell when you have a full stop.

Fast Fact

'Thanks' and 'Please' will always be the first word of a sentence. They will never follow a comma unless you have a word like 'and' after the comma before the 'thanks' or 'please'.

'However' can be written in the middle of sentences or at the beginning, but do get the punctuation right. The use of 'however' is shown correctly in both these examples:

- I am looking forward to going to China again next week. This time, however, I shall be speaking at a conference.
- I am looking forward to going to China again next week. However, this time I shall be speaking at a conference.

Electronic emotions

Although email is generally thought of as informal, it is unfortunately devoid of the non-verbal communication that is so often taken for granted in real conversations. Facial expressions, body language and voice inflections are often used in speech to convey a lot of our meaning. For example, consider how you might interpret the meanings of this statement as the speaking emphasis varies in each case:

YOU told him that?

You TOLD him that?

You told HIM that?

You told him THAT?

In personal email messages we can overcome the loss of this non-verbal expression by conveying emotions using emoticons. Another name for emoticons is 'smileys'. Very often, a picture is worth a thousand words. And we can use emoticons to liven up instant message conversations to let friends know how we are feeling.

I would not advise using emoticons in business email messages, but here are a few you might find useful in personal emails. There are, of course, many more.

Emoticon	Meaning
:-)	smile
:-(	sad
;-)	winking
:-P	sticking out your tongue
:-D	big delighted grin
:-|	no feelings either way
:-/	puzzled or confused
:-&	tongue-tied
:-O	yelling or completely shocked
:-[	fed up
:'-(	crying
:-()	can't (or won't) stop talking
8-O	amazed

FAST FACT

Emoticons were developed in the early days of chat rooms, forums and newsgroups as users began typing in the way we talk. Emoticons evolved out of a need to bring subtle inflections and tones into written communication. For example: *Our staff retreat next month will be held in Bali! Isn't that great news? ;-)*

Abbreviations

In personal email or in text messages, we often use abbreviations. These help people to cut down on typing. So many new abbreviations are being thought up all the time that it's often quite difficult to keep pace with them all. I also feel they can be overused and sometimes taken to extremes. However, I'm including a list of the most commonly used abbreviations in case you want to 'join the club'.

Abbreviation	Meaning
b4	before
BTW	by the way
CU	see you
F2F	face-to-face
FWIW	for what it's worth
FYI	for your information
IDK	I don't know
IMHO	in my humble opinion
JIC	just in case
L8R	later
LOL	laughing out loud
TIA	thanks in advance
TTYL	talk to you later

Danger Zone

Remember to use such abbreviations only when you are sure the recipient will understand them. And if you write to me, please don't use them at all!

Myth Buster

It's OK to use emoticons and abbreviations in business email messages. It helps to lighten things up, right?

My feeling is that it's rarely appropriate to use emoticons and abbreviations in business email. If you express yourself clearly in words and full sentences, your personality will shine through!

Before you hit 'Send'

Do you run the risk of causing yourself a great deal of damage through using email in an inappropriate way, or taking your email for granted? It's true that we are now sending more email messages than ever before. We even email people sitting at the next cubicle instead of walking a few steps. (Go on, admit it!) The problem is, this familiarity and convenience is encouraging us to nurture sloppy, dangerous habits — habits that can ruin our reputations!

Let's look at some facts:

- Careless email, especially if you slander someone, could land you in court.

- Email is never completely private. Something you wrote could come back to haunt you. Your message may also be posted on your company's notice board, or mailed to a competitor.

- Email messages can be used in legal investigations or as evidence in lawsuits.

- Email passwords can be stolen.

- Email messages are monitored by your IT department. It may cost you your job if you violate company policies.

- Careless and sloppy emailing can tarnish your reputation.

So before you hit 'Send' again, ask yourself these questions:

- Could I say this to the person's face?

- Am I violating any policies or laws?

- Would I want this message forwarded to someone else?

- Is the information in a logical order and easy to read?

- Am I writing this while I'm angry or upset?

- Will the reader know clearly what to do in response?

- Will my email give a good impression of me?

- Is email the best way to deliver this information?

- Is email more appropriate than a phone call or face-to-face communication?

- Will my email get the right results?

If your answers are 'Yes', you can now hit 'Send'!

STAR TIPS
for nurturing your email netiquette

1. Use emoticons and abbreviations only in personal email, text messages and instant messages.

2. Avoid using emoticons or abbreviations in business email.

3. Revisit the basic rules of grammar from time to time. Something as simple as an incorrect verb can leave your reader confused.

4. Help yourself and your reader by understanding where commas and other punctuation marks should be placed.

5. Read your messages out loud before sending. This is a good check to make sure your punctuation is in the right place.

6. Avoid subject/verb agreement errors by keeping your sentences short.

7. Get your message right the first time. Once you hit 'Send', it could be in the recipient's inbox within seconds.

8. Don't engage in unethical behaviour on the Internet.

9. Ask yourself if email is the best form of communication, or if a phone call might be better.

10. Take pride in your finished message. It gives the reader an impression of you, so make sure it's a good one.

4

LOOKING GOOD ONLINE

There is an invisible garment woven around us from our earliest years; it is made of the way we eat, the way we walk, the way we greet people.
— Jean Giraudoux

THERE ARE SIX STAGES we need to go through with every message. In this chapter we'll go through each of these stages to make sure that you get the details just right in all your email messages:

1. Tell your mail program that you want to send a new message.

2. Complete the address line.

3. Decide if you want to send anyone a copy or a blind copy.

4. Fill in the subject line.

5. Compose the message.

6. Send.

Seven deadly sins of message preparation

Read this list of seven deadly sins of message preparation and tick the ones that apply to you. If you tick a few of these items, you need help.

☐ You sometimes forget to include a subject heading. At other times you have trouble thinking up an appropriate and relevant heading.

☐ You often CC your email messages to lots of people without thinking whether they really need to see them.

☐ You sometimes send messages without a greeting or a closing section.

☐ You always use the same 'Regards' every time you finish an email.

☐ You haven't set up an automatic signature for your email.

☐ Your organisation has no standard disclaimer at the end of email messages.

☐ You sometimes forget to attach the file you said you would attach.

CC and BCC

Use the CC field for the addresses of those people who are not the main recipients of the message but who need to be kept informed. Use the BCC field for sending a blind copy (i.e. without the other recipients knowing about it). Both these features should be used sensibly. Near the top of the list of complaints from the people I surveyed is how it is so easy to click on the CC box and zap off copies of messages to anyone you wish. People who believe their correspondence with you is confidential may not be too happy if they find you've copied their messages to other people, since these may be people they had deliberately left off their original CC list!

Quickly double-check your CC and BCC boxes before you click 'Send'. Make sure they are exactly as you want them to be. It's too easy to hit the wrong key and 'Reply all' so that everyone on the original CC list ends up receiving a copy of your reply.

FAST FACT

For those too young to remember, CC originally meant 'carbon copy'. Those were the days when we had manual typewriters and backing sheets, and carbon paper was the only way of making duplicate copies of correspondence. Technological evolution has meant that carbon paper is a thing of the past, but CC has stuck — it has now come to mean 'courtesy copy', and BCC 'blind courtesy copy'.

SMART subject lines

Busy business people receive dozens of email messages every day, sometimes hundreds. It is a constant battle to capture the attention and interest of your readers. Too often writers compose subject lines that are far too vague, bland or too long to be effective. If you are guilty of any of these, then you need help with your subject lines. Do you ever:

- **Leave the subject field blank?** If so, your message may be identified as spam and sent to trash.

- **Use a previous email to write about something new, but you leave the old (unrelated) subject line in place?** If you insist on clicking 'Reply' to a previous email when writing about a new topic, please delete all the correspondence and type in the new subject line.

- **Type questions or your whole enquiry in the subject field and leave the message blank?** This is the height of laziness. The subject field is for a subject. The message field is for a message!

- **Type a bland or vague word or phrase in the subject field, which doesn't make it clear what the message is about?** 'Hello', 'Enquiry' or 'Latest info' will just not do. Nothing but a clear, specific subject line will work.

FAST FACT

Just like business people prioritise their workload, studies show that email recipients refer to the subject field to prioritise their emails, and more importantly, to determine whether or not they will open the email at all. Help your recipient by making it quite clear in your subject line exactly what your message is all about.

If you want to make sure your subject lines stand out, and so make sure your messages are read, you should aim to make them:

- Specific
- Meaningful
- Appropriate
- Relevant
- Thoughtful

Specific
Avoid vague or generic subject lines like 'Enquiry' or 'Information'. These are useless. Be very specific in your subject heading, while also being concise.

Meaningful
Make sure your subject line is explicit and meaningful. For example, sending a message to a technical support help desk with the heading 'Help Needed' is as good as having no heading at all.

Appropriate
Keep your subject line concise and to the point. It should be a brief summary of what the message is about, not an extract from it. It should also be professional and fitting for the purpose.

Relevant
Hit the nail on the head so that the reader is completely clear what you are writing about.

Thoughtful
Spare a thought for readers who may have 50 or more messages in their inbox. By composing a great subject line, you can help both the reader as well as yourself. Your subject line should indicate the context of the message at a glance. It is a good idea to limit your subject lines to 50 characters or about 5–7 words.

AHA! MOMENT
What I put in my subject line can often mean the difference between whether my message is read right now, today, tomorrow, next week or never!

When writing a subject line, think long-term

One important thing to think about regarding your subject line is this: will readers be able to find an email when they need it, perhaps weeks or months after receiving it?

Let's consider emailing out minutes of a meeting. You may receive lots of minutes. Make sure you compose a subject line that people can find when they need it. Perhaps:

> Subject: Fundraising Committee Minutes 21 March 2017

Here are four subject lines in my email inbox. Which would work for the long term?

> Subject: Hey Shirley

> Subject: Content calendar – for your approval

> Subject: Hi from Johnson Technology

> Subject: Important information on Leadership Challenge
> Seminar

If I were to keep these messages for several months, I believe 2 and 4 would still be easy to identify. Number 1 is probably spam, and number 3 identifies only the sender's company. Number 2 is easily found, and the title of the seminar in number 4 makes this also easily found.

FAST FACT
Before sending out an email, think of the future. If you are sending a policy, a procedure, a proposal, a list of resources, or other documents readers will want to keep, compose a subject that will make sense in a week, a month, or a year.

Examples of subject lines

Let's take a look at some good and some not-so-good subject lines:

1. This subject line is useless — it tells the reader nothing:

> Subject: Enquiry

This is more specific, giving the reader an idea of what the message is about:

> Subject: Enquiry about Gold Membership Plan

2. This message is OK but still not specific enough considering the content:

> Subject: Yahoto sale

This is more meaningful, concise and specific:

> Subject: 27 May — Closing date for Yahoto sale   ✓

3. This is rather vague:

> Subject: Quarterly results

This is much more descriptive:

> Subject: Second quarter results up by 20%   ✓

4. Your system may truncate subject lines that are more than a set length. This happens particularly with handhelds. Suppose this is what you want to put in your subject field: 'Important information on how to write subject lines that give your email messages some real oomph!' Here's what may appear in your subject field:

> Subject: Important information on how to write sub

Composing a precise and clear subject line takes practice. In this case, perhaps:

> Subject: Put some oomph into your subject line!

 MYTH BUSTER
We should always write in the subject line first, before
we write the message.
Says who? It may be better to write your subject line ✓
after you've written the message. Then you will be able to summarise the content more precisely in the subject line.

Keep your subject lines positive

Your subject line creates the 'mood' of your message. Warm up your message and set the right tone by creating positive subject lines.

Consider these:

Instead of:	Write:
New employee	Welcome Martha Tan to Sales
Meeting follow-up	Follow-up to our great meeting
Your reservation number 32282	Welcome to the Hampton Resort & Spa
Confusion re schedule	Clarification needed re schedule
Problems with department budget	Feedback on department budget

 DANGER ZONE
It's not OK to hit 'Reply' and keep the same subject heading if you are changing the subject. If you must click on 'Reply', please do two things: (1) change the subject line, and (2) delete the whole history of the previous conversation.

Greetings (or salutations)

Every new medium develops its own protocols for meeting and greeting as well as for closing. Telephone conversations start with 'Hello' and end with 'Bye'. Traditional business letters have always followed these formalities:

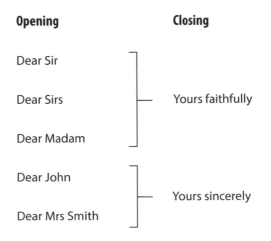

Opening	Closing
Dear Sir	
Dear Sirs	Yours faithfully
Dear Madam	
Dear John	
Dear Mrs Smith	Yours sincerely

These rules are too formal for email messages, and I would never suggest that anyone should end emails with 'Yours faithfully' or 'Yours sincerely'. However, it is still thought to be polite to begin and end emails with a greeting and a close. Some people choose to ignore this detail. They say it's quite clear who the message is to and from because of the automatic headers. However, when no greetings are included, a message can seem cold and the writer somewhat distant. Simple greetings are common courtesy, and this goes a long way. And after all, how long does it take? Are you really too busy to be courteous?

There are two good reasons for including a greeting:

- Readers can double-check that they are the intended recipient when they look at the greeting and see their own name.

- It clarifies the context in which they are receiving the message. For example, if the greeting does not bear your name you should look at the CC list to see if that's why you received the message.

The way you begin your email messages will depend on various factors:

- Your relationship with the recipient

- How frequently you communicate with the recipient

- How many recipients there are

- The status of the recipient — you will address your CEO very differently from how you address your colleague in the next office

- Your personal style and preference

- Your company's preferred style

That said, the way business is conducted in general now is much more informal than in the past. Business meetings are much less formal than they used to be. First names are now widely used rather than full formal titles. The same informality is also common in business writing and emailing.

If you would greet someone with a first name face-to-face, then do the same in email:

Dear Kelvin

If you would greet someone more formally in person, then do the same in email:

Dear Mr Long

When the recipient replies to you, take a good look at the way he or she signs off at the end of the message. If the recipient has addressed you by your first name and has signed off as 'Iris Tan', then next time you write you may begin with 'Dear Iris'.

If you are writing to a group of people you can say 'Dear' plus the group name:

Dear All

Dear Marketing Executives

Dear Supervisors

Dear Manchester United Fans

If you are writing to someone you know very well and/or communicate with regularly, 'Dear' may be a bit too formal. You may want to begin with the more informal 'Hi' or 'Hello':

Hello Mark

Hi Sally

Greetings across cultures

Salutations can be tricky across cultures where sometimes the family name is first and sometimes last, or sometimes there are three or four names and you aren't sure which one you should use when you greet them. It can be frustrating trying to decide on an appropriate greeting in your email, especially if you can't even tell if the person is male or female.

TRY THIS

If you find yourself emailing someone whose name you aren't sure about, here are a few suggestions as to what you could do:

- Call up the Consulate for that particular country and ask for their advice.
- Ask a colleague or friend who has lived in the country where your reader is from.
- Call up the reception of the person's company and ask them how to address this person.
- Call up the person him/herself, introduce yourself, and ask them how you should address them. This personal contact will definitely go a long way towards building better bonds even before you email them. Learn more about building better relationships in Chapter 7.

FAST FACT

Greetings like 'Good morning' or 'Good afternoon' don't really make much sense with email. You never know when your recipient will open his or her mail, especially when communicating across time zones.

Ending your message

There are various thoughts about how to finish an email message. I have never been a fan of ending with 'Regards'. It seems so cold and unemotional, even quite meaningless to me. However, I can see that this is one of the most popular closings, so on this issue I have to hold my hands up and submit. So if you feel comfortable with it, go ahead and end your email messages with 'Regards'. But you'll never receive a message from me with that ending! Let's look at some alternatives.

If it suits your personality, for more informal messages or with people you know really well, you may choose something like:

> Cheers

If you have been writing to ask someone to do something, it may be appropriate to finish with:

> Many thanks

On some occasions a close with a little more feeling may be appropriate:

> Best wishes
>
> All the best
>
> Good luck!
>
> See you soon

Here are some other popular closings:

> Best
>
> Warmly
>
> Take care

You could also end with phrases that reflect the purpose of your email, in which case you really don't need anything else, such as:

Have a great day.

Enjoy your weekend.

Happy Holidays!

To your success.

When you use closes like these, you really don't need 'Regards'. Go on, I dare you, stop the 'Regards' right now!

FAST FACT
Your closing is really just the icing on the cake. Your main message is what will really set the whole tone of your message, so that's the most important section. But by choosing an appropriate sign-off, you are giving just one more sign of what a great pleasure it's going to be communicating with you.

Signatures

There are two good reasons for a sign-off or signature section:

- Without a sign-off, your recipient will have no other information about you except your email address. If you have included a sign-off or signature, then your recipient will be able to address you correctly.

- A sign-off section lets your recipient know that they have reached the end of your message. It is not uncommon for email transmissions to be interrupted, so at least if you have signed off appropriately you know your reader will not be left wondering, 'Is that all?'

Include your job title, the name of your organisation and your contact details. Telephone numbers are particularly important things to include because the recipient may actually want to discuss the matter with you over a phone call. Do remember that whenever any of the details change you must revise your signature details to ensure everything is up-to-date.

Here's a detailed signature:

> Shirley Taylor, CSP
> CEO, STTS Training Pte Ltd
> 02-01 Orchid Towers, 88 Victoria Park Lane,
> Singapore 236273
> Tel: +65 6231 4810
> Company website: www.sttstraining.com
> Shirley's website: www.shirleytaylor.com
> Follow me on: Facebook | LinkedIn | Twitter

For people who know you better and have all your details, or for personal emails, you may want to include your personal contact details or a website address:

> Shirley Taylor
> Website: www.shirleytaylor.com
> Telephone +65 6231 4810

MYTH BUSTER

People expect to see advertising messages and images too as part of your signature file.

Not necessarily! Don't make the mistake of thinking that everyone wants to read another entire paragraph of your ad material. Keep your signature file short with essentials only. Don't scare people off with too much information.

Fun final thought on greetings and closings

In one of my workshops, a man was very adamant that he didn't need to use a greeting or a closing. 'You know it's for you, it's in your mailbox. You know it's from me, it says so! I finish all my messages with "Cheers" and nothing else.' We couldn't make him agree that he needed his name at the end, so we just moved on. The second morning he walked into the room laughing, and told me, 'Shirley, I have a lot of correspondence from Japan, and last night I opened my mail and one

message began, "Dear Mr Cheers".' I think from that day onwards, this man has always put his name at the end of his messages!

Disclaimers and confidentiality clauses

Whether your email messages should include a disclaimer and/or confidentiality notice is a matter that must be considered by companies individually. From a legal point of view it may be advisable to do so. Some companies have different disclaimers for internal and external messages, but what may begin as an internal message may be copied externally. This must be considered when composing disclaimer notices.

Here are some examples of disclaimers:

This email is confidential and intended for the addressee only. If you are not the person to whom it is addressed, you must not print, copy or distribute it or take any action on it. Email may be intercepted or corrupted and XYZ Company is unable to accept responsibility for any breach of confidence arising through use of this medium. XYZ Company will not accept liability for contractual commitments or statements made by individuals employed by this company outside the scope of our business.

XYZ Company does not accept legal responsibility for the contents of this message. Any views or opinions presented are solely those of the author and do not necessarily represent those of XYZ Company.

This email may be confidential and privileged. Any form of unauthorised use is prohibited. If it has been wrongly sent to you, please delete it immediately and notify the sender.

FAST FACT

Disclaimers are becoming more and more complex. But keep in mind that legally they offer only limited protection, no matter how long and complicated they are!

Attachments

One of the most useful features of email is the ability to attach files. This allows people to share any file in any format — images, Word documents, Excel spreadsheets, PowerPoint presentations, audio-visual files, data files, and so on. If something can be saved as an electronic file, it can be sent along with your email message. This works very well when:

- You remember to attach the file

- Your reader has the software to open the file

- The attachment does not contain a virus

DANGER ZONE

I'm sure you've been guilty more than once of sending an email without the attachment, so you have to send another one saying, 'Oops, I forgot to attach this'. This is a common and easily made mistake, but it can be annoying if it happens too often. Why not make a point to attach the file before you start typing the message? Alternatively, when you type the part of the message that says the file is attached, stop immediately and attach the file. This works for me.

File format for attachments

Attachments can cause frustration for some recipients, especially if they cannot open the file. One of the main reasons for this is that the recipient does not have the same version of the software that you use. If this happens you can often spend ages sending email back and forth saying, 'It didn't work — can you try sending it again?' Before sending a file, if you are in any doubt at all it's best to send a simple email asking if the recipient can accept attachments easily.

Zip it up

Downloading large files can sometimes take a long time as well as take up a lot of space. Software is available that compresses files (e.g. WinZip or StuffIt) but you need to ensure that your recipient has the software to decompress them at the other end. WinZip also allows you to send as many files as you want to attach as a single compressed file.

Post the attachment instead

An alternative to attaching files to internal emails is to post the file on an intranet server and tell your recipients where the file can be found. The recipients can then decide if and when they want to look at it, and then whether or not they will download it onto their own workstation. This can be particularly useful, for instance, when you inform members about a staff meeting. You can post all the presentation materials on your intranet, then send a message to all participants with the URL (and possibly the password if the documents are confidential). They can then download whatever documents they need or want.

 MYTH BUSTER

Sending a 'Recall last message' email will stop people reading your mail.

Sorry! Sending people an email asking them not to read the email you just sent them is an invitation for them to read it. Get your message right by checking it carefully before you hit 'Send'.

STAR TIPS
for looking good online

1. If you want to ensure your message is opened and read, a SMART subject line is essential.

2. Include an appropriate greeting and closing section on all your messages.

3. Use an automatic signature and change it when appropriate.

4. Don't be tempted to click 'Reply all' unless it's really essential that everyone sees the message.

5. Send a CC only to people who really need to read the email.

6. Remember to include some niceties at the end of messages, such as 'Good luck', 'Have a great weekend', etc.

7. Check your messages carefully before hitting 'Send'.

8. Proofreading means a lot more than running spellcheck.

9. Attachments are great, but only when you remember to attach them.

10. Remember, email conversations come to an end too.

5

WRITING GREAT EMAILS

If you can't explain it simply, you don't understand it well enough.
— Albert Einstein

YOUR MESSAGE IS the most important part of any email, so it's important to make sure you say what you want to say in modern business language and appropriate tone, and make sure it looks good. That way it has a greater chance of being effective.

Effective communication gives a professional impression of you and your organisation and helps to get things done. It seems we are now writing more than ever, and very often speed is the key to successful negotiations. Writing effectively under these circumstances can be very challenging.

In this chapter we will be looking at ways you can improve your written communication, even in the most demanding circumstances, so that your messages are effective and achieve the desired results.

Seven deadly sins of business writing

Read this list of seven deadly sins of business writing and tick the ones that apply to you. If you tick a few of these items, you need help. This chapter will help you write great emails that get the right results.

- ☐ You use language in business communication that is more suited to your great-grandparents.

- ☐ You use lots of old-fashioned or unnecessary words and expressions just because other people always use them.

- ☐ You spend a lot of time thinking of what to say and trying to get your messages just right.

- ☐ You have long email conversations back and forth with people trying to clarify things and answer more questions.

- ☐ You write brief messages that sometimes come over as cold and unfeeling.

- ☐ You don't know the difference between active and passive voice.

- ☐ Some people tell you that your tone in emails is very abrupt.

Top 10 complaints about email in practice

I was very grateful to many people who responded to a survey that I carried out asking them to share with me their main complaints about email in practice. Here are some common complaints that I heard. If you use email regularly I'm sure you will be nodding your head in agreement with some of these.

1. Vague subject line

People will sometimes not even read a message unless the subject line captures their attention in the first place. Busy people with lots of messages every day just do not have the time. Help your reader to understand the bigger picture by composing a clear subject line that tells the reader exactly what the message is all about. Your subject line should be brief (many mailers will cut off long subject lines) and should give the essence of the content of the message. See SMART subject lines in Chapter 4.

 DANGER ZONE
A message that is sent with an empty subject line or one that says 'Help me!' or 'Urgent' will probably end up in the recipient's trash. A good subject line will not only help the recipient, it will also help you by ensuring your message is read.

2. No greeting and no sign-off

Nothing annoys me more than receiving a message from someone that doesn't begin with a simple greeting or end with the name of the sender. Please remember the simple courtesies of a greeting and sign-off. You can see more about what's acceptable in Chapter 4.

3. Just plain sloppy

As more people use email, sloppy work is becoming more of a problem. Common complaints include:

- Not being clear on the goal of the email

- Not attempting to structure the message logically

- Not doing spellcheck

- Using text-like code and abbreviations

- Poor typing habits

- Not stating the action required, leaving the reader wondering

4. Using the wrong case

Sloppy work sometimes results in writers using ALL CAPITALS or lower case abbreviations. In the world of email, using capital letters is equivalent to SHOUTING! (Didn't you automatically raise your voice then, even when reading this to yourself?) Capitals are seen as rude and annoying, and it should not be necessary even to put a subject line in capital letters. At the other extreme, some people cannot be bothered with capital letters at all, and this can be very frustrating, as can abbreviations like the ones seen in the following message. Sometimes a message can be abbreviated so much that it is difficult to read.

> To: shirley@shirleytaylortraining.com
>
> Subject: HELLO!!!
>
> hi Shirley, I hope things are well with u.
>
> its good 2 know that u will be back in Malaysia again in nov to hold your seminar on effective biz writing. pls would u let me have some free date while u r over here, some bookstores r interested in a talk cum singing event and I hope you will agree 2 take part.
>
> tnks & rgds
>
> Kiri

MYTH BUSTER

We can use capitals to emphasise important sections of our email messages.

Please don't. Apart from being more difficult to read, capital letters imply shouting and aggression. SO DON'T USE CAPITALS FOR ANY PART OF YOUR MESSAGE! also pls don't use lower case letters with abbreviations n acronyms. If u write this way u r thot of as lazy and I 4 one wouldn't want that, wld u? Find out more about things like this in Chapter 3.

5. Bad grammar, spelling and punctuation

A quick way to lower your credibility is to send out messages with spelling, punctuation or grammar errors. Remember that your messages give an impression of your organisation and of you as an individual. Make sure it is a good impression by taking as much care when composing an email message as you would with a formal letter. For more advice on sprucing up your cyber-grammar skills, see Chapter 3.

6. Poor formatting

Some people just ramble on and on in their messages, with no spaces or breaks between paragraphs. Talk about showing no respect for the reader's time or ease of understanding! If you write long-winded sentences with no paragraphing and no blank lines between paragraphs, your message will not be easy to read, and that will not do your reputation any good. For help in putting together an effective message, see Chapter 9.

7. Vague messages

In my survey, many people commented that they received messages in which it was difficult to figure out what action was needed. Email messages are often sent in such a rush that the writer does not plan the message beforehand and makes no effort to structure it properly. Other writers ramble on in lengthy paragraph after lengthy paragraph so that eventually they miss the point altogether. Such messages rarely achieve their objectives and will only frustrate and confuse.

8. Unfriendly tone

The most difficult thing to convey in email is emotions. This often gets people into trouble because they type out exactly what they would say without thinking of the tone of voice that would be used to signal their emotions. It is therefore easy for misunderstandings to occur in email. When sending email, remember that readers could be put on the defensive if your tone is not quite right. Learn more about touching up your tone in Chapter 8.

9. CC the whole world

Email users often complain that they are sent copies of email messages just for the sake of it, or are forwarded copies of long messages that they don't really need to see. Think very carefully about who needs to see a copy of your email message. Send messages to everyone who needs to know, not to everyone you know!

10. Hunting for the response

Something else that is quite annoying is when you have sent a message to someone, and in replying their response is placed at the end of the original message instead of at the top. As a result, you open the email and the first thing you see is your own message, so your first thought is confusion, then it hits you that the sender's message may be somewhere else, so you have to go hunting around looking for the reply. Please don't waste people's time like this. Format your default so your messages are at the top when you click 'Reply'.

Four rules for great email writing

Here is what you need to remember when writing business documents. These rules apply to composing any written message, not just emails.

Rule 1: Avoid redundant phrases

A lot of messages are filled with long-winded jargon. Busy business people welcome messages that are straight to the point while retaining courtesy. Save the recipient's time by keeping sentences short and simple, and by avoiding long-winded, old-fashioned language. For example:

> ✗ Please be informed that a management meeting will be held on Monday 12 July 2018.
> ✓ **A management meeting will be held on Monday 12 July 2018.**

> ✗ Please be informed that this order will be despatched to you on 12 July.
> ✓ **This order will be sent to you on 12 July.**

> ✗ Please note that the fire alarms will be tested next Thursday 7 April.
> ✓ **The fire alarms will be tested next Thursday 7 April.**

TRY THIS

Throw these redundant phrases in your trash bin, and never use them again:

✗ I would like to bring to your attention that ...

✗ I would like to take this opportunity to ...

✗ I would like to inform you that ...

✗ Thank you for your kind attention.

✗ Thank you in anticipation.

Rule 2: Keep it short and simple (KISS)

The essence of good business writing is to keep to the essentials. Busy business people don't have time to read long rambling messages. Say what you want to say in the quickest possible way, while retaining courtesy of course.

When composing email messages make sure you remember your KISSing. KISS means simplify your words and phrases as in these examples:

Instead of:	Write:
commence	start
despatch	send
utilise	use
purchase	buy
visualise	see
assist	help
sufficient	enough
prior to	before
in view of the fact that	as, since
in the event that	if
conduct an investigation	investigate
We would like to ask you to	Please

Keeping it short and simple also means avoiding unnecessary words and expressions. There are many frequently used words that add nothing to the message. These words could easily be removed without changing the meaning. Here are some words and phrases to cut out of your writing:

- ✗ all things being equal
- ✗ as a matter of fact
- ✗ at the end of the day
- ✗ at this moment in time
- ✗ basically
- ✗ in due course
- ✗ in other words
- ✗ in this connection
- ✗ last but not least
- ✗ each and every one
- ✗ the fact of the matter is
- ✗ for all intents and purposes
- ✗ I would like to take this opportunity

Fast Fact

I'm often asked how long a sentence should be. Here is what I usually recommend: In letters, memos and emails, use an average sentence length of 10–15 words. In formal reports and technical documents, keep the average sentence length to 15–20 words.

Rule 3: Use modern language

Today's business language should be as natural as possible, as if you were having a conversation. Here are some examples of old-fashioned business language that has been updated to a more natural, conversational style:

Instead of:	Write:
Referring to your message of 23 May.	Thanks for your message of 23 May.
Attached herewith please find ...	Attached is ... I attach ... Here is ...
Please advise me ...	Please let me know ...
I should be grateful if you would be good enough to advise me ...	Please let me know ...
Please favour us with a prompt reply.	I look forward to your prompt reply.
We seek your assistance to forward to us the additional premium of S$15.62 at your earliest convenience. Kindly note that payment should reach us by 28 November 2018.	Please let us have your cheque for S$15.62 by 28 November 2018.
As per our discussion, I will speak to my colleague Jonathan Long and request that he sends you our quotation as soon as possible.	My colleague, Jonathan Long, will send you our quotation soon.
Should you require any further clarifications please do not hesitate to contact me.	Please give me a call if you have any questions.

Rule 4: Consider your reader

Empathy is an important quality to remember in all business dealings. This is particularly so when sending email messages. When reading through your email before sending it, make sure you empathise with your reader. This means imagining how they will feel as they read your message. Ask yourself these questions:

- Will the reader find your message clear and well written?

- Have you written confidently and positively?

- Have you obtained the right balance between formality and informality while retaining courtesy?

- Will they be confused, annoyed or feel that you have wasted their time?

- Does your email convey a good impression?

- Is the language appropriate or over their head?

- Could anything be considered insensitive or distasteful?

When you have put yourself in the reader's shoes and considered your message carefully, it may be necessary to reword the message more appropriately or restructure it so that it achieves a smooth transition from one idea to the next.

The golden rule: write as you speak

I am always amazed at some of the emails I receive using language like: 'Please kindly peruse the above-mentioned document', 'Appreciate your kind assistance in this matter', or 'The said report is attached herewith for your reference and perusal'.

When my workshop participants ask me if they can use such language, my answer is always: 'Would you say it if you were speaking to someone?' They always laugh and say, 'No!' And there lies the golden rule of writing: If you wouldn't say it, don't write it!

Check out these sentences that we often see in emails, and consider their modern equivalents:

✗ We refer to your email message.
✓ **Thanks for your email.**

✗ The above-mentioned workshop will be held next Tuesday, 4 May.
✓ **This workshop will be held next Tuesday, 4 May.**

✗ The below-mentioned goods will be despatched to you next Monday.
✓ **These goods will be sent to you next Monday.**

✗ Please furnish me with this information at your soonest.
✓ **Please let me have this information soon.**

✗ Kindly revert to me asap.
✓ **I hope to hear from you soon.**

✗ Please find attached herewith a copy of our latest catalogue for your reference and perusal.
✓ **I am attaching our latest catalogue, and I hope you find it interesting.**

MYTH BUSTER

Many of my workshop participants say to me, 'I use a very informal style when I speak to people, but when I write to them I have to use a more formal style, right?'

Wrong! Why do we need a different language for writing? It's the 21st century and we need to write as though we are speaking for it to sound natural, not in a fake way that takes too much effort and sounds totally insincere.

Compose CLEAR messages

You can ensure your email messages are effective if you follow these CLEAR guidelines:

- Compact
- Logical
- Empathetic
- Action-based
- Right

Compact
Einstein once said, 'Everything should be as simple as possible, but no simpler.' Keep your message brief and concise, with short sentences, in straightforward conversational language. This will be easier for you to write and for your readers to read and understand.

Logical
Remember that all good messages begin with an opening, then continue with the main details, and lead naturally to an action statement. (Check out my Four-Point Plan in Chapter 9.)

Empathetic

Respect your readers, identify with them, appreciate their feelings. In this way you will ensure that your message is written in words they will understand and in an appropriate tone.

Action-based

Explain exactly what you want your readers to do or how you wish them to respond, then they are more likely to do so.

Right

Make sure your message is correct in terms of grammar, spelling and punctuation, and that it includes all essential facts and details.

 ## TRY THIS

Next time you are tempted to write these phrases, change them as shown here:

Instead of:	*Write:*
Appreciate if you would ...	Please ...
Please be reminded...	Please remember ...
The above-mentioned order ...	This order ...
Please find attached ...	I am attaching ...

 ## MYTH BUSTER

Many people tell me that following these 'Keep it simple' guidelines is one thing when you are just writing simple messages, but they find that keeping messages short and simple can easily come across as blunt and abrupt.

Is it possible to be brief but still retain courtesy? With effort, yes. It's very important to use the right tone and style in your writing. You will find lots of examples of this in Chapter 8.

Yesterday's versus today's business writing

In my email writing workshops, I'm always amazed at how many young people use so many old-fashioned expressions. Why is this? On the one hand we keep up-to-date with new technology, new computer programs and software. Yet on the other hand we often use language and expressions more suited to our great-grandparents. This is such an irony!

Not too many decades ago, business writing was formal, long-winded, pompous and serious. Take a look at this letter, which may have been written several decades ago. Go through it and highlight all the old-fashioned phrases and outdated words, passive phrases and redundancies.

> Dear Sir,
>
> We have received your letter dated 27th March.
>
> We are extremely distressed to learn that an error was made pertaining to your esteemed order. The cause of your complaint has been investigated, and it actually appears that the error occurred in our packing section, but it was not discerned before the order was despatched to your goodself.
>
> Kindly be informed that arrangements have been made for a repeat order to be despatched to you immediately, and this should leave our warehouse later today.
>
> Enclosed herewith please find a copy of our new catalogue for your reference and perusal.

> Should you have any further queries, please do not hesitate to contact the undersigned.
>
> Thank you for your kind attention.
>
> Yours faithfully,
>
> Zachariah Creep & Partners

If you were looking for all the points I asked you to look for, virtually the entire letter would be highlighted by now.

The way business is conducted has changed immensely over the last few decades, even more so in the last few years. Informality is now the key. Writing styles have also changed tremendously. The aim in modern business communication is to write in a friendly, informal style using plain language, as if you are having a conversation. See how different today's approach is in this email:

Dear Mr Tan

Thank you for your email.

I am sorry to hear about the mistake with your order. This error happened in our packing section, and unfortunately it was not noticed before the goods were sent to you.

A repeat order will be sent to you immediately. It should leave our warehouse today.

I am attaching our latest catalogue, which I'm sure you will find interesting. Please call me on 6454545 if you have any questions.

Once again, my apologies for the inconvenience.

Lena Cheng

Did you spot the differences in the second one? Did you notice the short sentences and active phrases instead of passive ones, simple words instead of lengthy ones, and the absence of redundancies and old-fashioned phrases?

Our great-grandfathers used very long-winded, bombastic writing many decades ago, just like in the first example. This is just not appropriate for the 21st century. Today's writing must be straightforward, simple, brief, and courteous — but definitely not bombastic!

You will not develop your own writing style overnight. Practise the skill of choosing words and constructing sentences and paragraphs. Take pride in your work and seek ways to improve it constantly. Learn how to be critical, and notice when something is well written and when it is badly written. Find a mode of expression that suits you.

Writing with heart

As you can see in the examples of yesterday's and today's business writing, there is a huge difference between how our ancestors used to write several decades ago and what our writing should look like today. But decades ago, life was also very different. People were more formal in their business and personal relationships, so they built relationships much more slowly. Their spoken language and tone matched their written language and tone.

Over the years, a lot has changed. Business and personal interactions are more informal now. We use a friendly, natural style in face-to-face meetings. As a result, we build relationships much quicker. However, has this translated into the same friendly, natural style in our writing? In many cases, no. Why is this? Why are many people still using a style in writing that is completely different from the way they speak? It just doesn't make sense.

More than ever today, writing is the lifeblood of your career success. If you are like most people, you will be emailing and texting and instant messaging more than you speak on the telephone or in person. You have written business relationships with people you have never met or rarely speak to.

With so much focus on writing, it is a challenge to write what we need to write in an appropriate way without ruining working relationships. Clumsy wording, template phrases, poor punctuation, passive/distant language and poor punctuation could unintentionally send the wrong message.

If you want to develop great relationships and enhance your success, you need to communicate with heart. You need to write with heart.

FAST FACT
Writing with heart means using natural language that connects with readers, develops great relationships and builds trust. Writing with heart means using relationship-building language that warms up your message.

Let's again look at the difference between writing yesterday and today by using adjectives that describe each style:

Yesterday	Today
cold	warm
distant	close
formal	informal
unfriendly	friendly
long-winded	brief
verbose	clear
pompous	unaffected
complicated	simple
template-style	conversational

Benefits of great writing

Using the tips and tools in this book will help you to:

- **Save time.** Your reader will not have to think about what you mean. It will be crystal clear. You will also save time writing and thinking about how to write.

- **Avoid confusion.** Your reader will know exactly what you are saying and how to respond without having to send you an email or call you to clarify.

- **Connect with people in a positive, natural way.** You'll create win-win relationships, which will lead to more sales and more opportunities..

- **Create a good impression.** A well-written message will make the reader think well not only of you but also of your organisation.

- **Enhance relationships.** You will develop a good relationship one message at a time.

- **Achieve the desired results.** You will communicate clearly, politely and powerfully, in a way that your reader will know exactly what action is needed.

STAR TIPS
for writing great emails

1. Learn the difference between today's business language and old-fashioned jargon.

2. Come straight to the point in messages while retaining courtesy and clarity.

3. Remember the KISS principle in all your written messages. Keep it short and simple.

4. Avoid redundant phrases like 'Please be informed' and 'I am writing to inform you'.

5. Write as if you are having a conversation with the recipient, using everyday language that you would use if you were speaking.

6. Make sure all your email messages are CLEAR: Compact, Logical, Empathetic, Action-based, and Right.

7. Aim to give a good impression of yourself and your organisation.

8. Consider your reader and his/her point of view when you write

9. Read carefully as though you are the reader, and consider how the reader will feel.

10. Pick up the phone when you know an email exchange is getting long.

6

THE POWER OF PLAIN ENGLISH

Using plain English is not just a good intention. It is a business necessity.

— Lord Alexander of Weedon, former NatWest Chairman

WITH LIMITED TIME and so much mail in our inboxes, readers want to read messages that are simple and clear. Readers want to read and understand messages easily, and know exactly how to reply.

If your readers are confused or can't focus when reading your messages, you could be missing out on countless business opportunities. Writing in plain English will mean you can click 'Send' with confidence, and your reader will easily understand what you're saying. And that means you are more likely to get the right response.

Seven deadly sins of plain English

Read this list of seven deadly sins of plain English and tick the ones that apply to you. If you tick a few of these items, you need help.

☐ You think using big words and long sentences will impress your readers.

☐ You think using a long phrase is better than one word.

☐ You think it's fine to use abbreviations, jargon and management buzzwords.

☐ You use phrases like 'Please be informed' at the beginning of some sentences.

☐ You think making your writing formal and complicated will impress readers.

☐ You don't know the difference between passive and active voice.

☐ You avoid using 'You' and 'I' because you think they're too casual for email.

If you answered yes to any of these questions, you may be making your business writing much more difficult than it should be. And more importantly, you're making reading much more difficult for your reader. You need to use plain English.

What is plain English?

If your message is important, then you will want to do everything you can to make sure that readers understand it. Plain English will help you. Plain English is writing that's fuss-free. It's easy to read, and easy to understand. Plain English involves using short, clear sentences with simple, everyday words. Plain English contains no redundancies or jargon.

I'm really happy to see that more organisations are taking action to simplify their language in official business documents and messages. Plain English is:

- Faster to write and faster to read

- Easier to understand

- Straight to the point, and also courteous

- Much more friendly

Benefits of plain English

1. Plain English is precise. Writers often think they should use formal language, lengthy sentences and bombastic words. However, all this increases the chance of misunderstanding.

2. Plain English is clear and unambiguous. Studies show that plain English can increase understanding by as much as 90 per cent.

3. Plain English is readable. Readers can absorb and understand the message in one reading. So many people dress up language to sound authoritative, but this can be ineffective as far as readability is concerned.

4. Plain English is brief. Many people could reduce their messages by up to one-third. This will save you time and money, and it will save your reader time too.

5. Plain English shows responsibility. Old-fashioned, passive writing very often shows no responsibility. Today it's so important to use active voice.

6. Plain English makes you more credible. People are more likely to trust you and build relationships with you if you use plain English.

FAST FACT

A study by the UK's Royal Mail estimated that British businesses lose up to £5 billion a year because of pretentious, inappropriate or error-filled writing.

The Plain English Campaign

Since 1979, the Plain English Campaign has been campaigning against gobbledygook, jargon and misleading public information. Based in the UK, they have helped many government departments and other official organisations with their documents, reports and publications. You can find out more about the Plain English Campaign and obtain their free guides at www.plainenglish.co.uk.

I love this quote shown on the Plain English Campaign website. It is extracted from a letter from Kensington Palace in 1994:

'Due to a frequent regrettable inability to prevent my presence in other locations, I find that I must convey to you my goodwill in a correspondence format. It was when I was still a juvenile future constitutional figurehead substitute that I first became sensitised by mother-tongue abuse awareness. How many of use, I wonder, when faced with pretentious gobbledygook and empty jargon, experience a kick start into despair mode? My feelings towards all of you at today's Awards are, attitudinally, those of enormous encouragement... God bless the Plain English Campaign.' — Charles, Prince of Wales

FAST FACT

When Arizona's Department of Revenue rewrote one letter in plain English, it received about 11,000 fewer phone calls than in the previous year.

Plain English means using active voice

Passive voice is vague and puts a distance between you and your reader. It makes your sentences much longer, and it doesn't show any responsibility.

- Passive voice means the subject *does the action of the sentence*.

- Active voice means the subject of the sentence *receives the action*.

Examples:

Passive	Active
The study was completed by the Marketing Director.	**The Marketing Director completed the study.**
Separate requisitions should be prepared by each buyer.	**Each buyer should prepare separate requisitions.**

In these examples of passive voice, you'll see that the 'person' in each sentence is at the end of the sentence. In the active sentence, the person comes first. Always aim to put the person first in your sentences. Here are some more examples of changing passive to active voice:

✗ Your order was received by us today.

✓ **Thank you for your order, which we received today.**

✗ The seminar was conducted by Robert Sim.

✓ **Robert Sim conducted the seminar.**

✗ A cheque should be obtained from your client.

✓ **Please ask your client for a cheque.**

✗ The monthly results were not included in your report.

✓ **You did not include the monthly results in your report.**

✗ The project was discussed by the managers at the monthly meeting.

✓ **The managers discussed the project at the monthly meeting.**

✗ The signed employment contract should be returned by 14 April.

✓ **Please return the signed employment contract by 14 April.**

✗ If the goods have not been received by next Friday, our transport department should be contacted immediately.

✓ **Please contact our transport department if you do not receive the goods by next Friday.**

Try This

Be on the lookout for passive sentences when you are reading other people's messages. Becoming aware in this way will help you to be more careful in using active voice in your own writing.

Using active voice can considerably improve your writing style. It will:

- Make the tone much more interesting and lively

- Sound more personal and natural

- Put people back into your writing

- Show ownership and responsibility

- Make your writing clear, specific and focused

- Make your writing shorter

Plain English focuses on verbs

The purpose of writing is to get things done. We often report on problems and solutions. We may update managers on projects and deadlines. We may have to present information, or request information.

If you want to help get things done, you need to keep your language simple, easy to read and easy to understand. One great way of doing this is to use one simple verb — or action — wherever possible.

Our ancestors used a lot of nominalisations in their writing. A nominalisation is a noun phrase generated from a verb. Nominalisations are often referred to as 'hidden verbs'. Like passive verbs, too many nominalisations make writing very dull and heavy-going.

Let's look at some examples, and their verb equivalents:

Nominalisation	Verb
come to a conclusion	conclude
made a decision	decided
undertake an investigation	investigate
made an improvement	improved

Let's look at some more examples:

✗ The neighbours finally agreed about the building of the fence.

✓ **The neighbours finally agreed to build a fence.**

✗ The committee will undertake an investigation into the reason for the damaged fire door.

✓ **The committee will investigate the reason for the damaged fire door.**

✗ We need to carry out a review of the department's processes so we can gain an understanding of the reason this error occurred.

✓ **We need to review the department's processes so we can understand why this error occurred.**

Aha! Moment

When I start using more verbs in my writing, I will avoid clutter, making my messages easier to read and understand.

Plain English means using 'you' and 'we'

It really helps to refer to the reader as 'you', rather than using words like 'the candidate' or 'the vendor'. You wouldn't use such words if the person was sitting across the desk from you, so don't use them in writing.

Here are some examples:

✗ Candidates must complete this form and return it to us.
✓ **Will you please complete this form and return it to us.**

✗ Advice is available at any time from our Support Hotline.
✓ **You can get advice at any time from our Support Hotline.**

✗ All customers must send us...
✓ **Could you please send us** or **Please send us...**

✗ It will be processed as soon as we hear from you.
✓ **We will process this as soon as we hear from you.**

P.S. It's quite alright to use 'we' and 'I' in the same message.

Fast Fact

Plain English also means:
- Using lists and bullets where appropriate
- Using simple words
- Avoiding redundant phrases

Plain English does not contain clichés and buzz phrases

A cliché is a phrase or expression that has been used so often that it is no longer original or interesting. These overused phrases can be a real barrier to communication because listeners often tune out when they hear one of these tired expressions. Here are a few clichés that I suggest you avoid:

- ✗ at the end of the day
- ✗ at this moment in time
- ✗ ballpark figure
- ✗ bottom line
- ✗ game plan
- ✗ going forward
- ✗ I hear what you're saying
- ✗ it's not rocket science
- ✗ think outside the box
- ✗ with all due respect

A buzz word or phrase is typically used to make something seem more impressive than it actually is. Let's look at some of these:

- ✗ 24/7
- ✗ bring it to the table
- ✗ circle back
- ✗ in the loop
- ✗ mission critical
- ✗ move the goalposts
- ✗ my people will talk to your people
- ✗ paradigm shift
- ✗ ride the wave
- ✗ take it to the next level

It's often thought that many of the staff at large organisations use management speak like this as a way of disguising the fact that they haven't done their job properly. Some people think they can bluff their way through by using long, impressive-sounding words and phrases, even if they don't really know what they mean.

FAST FACT

You can find many more examples of clichés and buzz words and phrases on the internet. There are also some fun games like Buzzword Bingo.

Quick check to make sure you are using plain English

Here's a checklist so you can check if your messages meet plain English standards. Ideally, you should be able to tick off all these points for every message you write:

☐ I have written this message with the reader in mind.

☐ I have used simple, everyday words.

☐ I have not used long sentences with gaps between subject, verb and object.

☐ I have structured my message logically.

☐ I have used appropriate headings.

☐ I have used lists and bullets where appropriate.

☐ I have used 'you' and other pronouns.

☐ I have used active voice.

☐ I have not used hidden verbs (nominalisations).

☐ I have written as though I am speaking, in a natural style.

☐ I have checked that my writing is helpful, polite and human.

FAST FACT

After producing a clearer bill in plain English, British Telecom saw customer enquiries fall by 25 per cent each quarter. Customers also paid their bills more promptly, which improved revenue and reduced the cost of collecting overdue bills. Before the change, BT had received a million calls a year.

STAR TIPS
for using plain English

1. Learn everything you can about plain English. It's the key to good business writing.

2. Use active voice to keep sentences shorter and more focused.

3. Avoid nominalisations (hidden verbs), which make your writing dull, heavy and lengthy.

4. Use pronouns like 'you' and 'we' in your messages.

5. Avoid clichés and buzz phrases.

6. Use simple, everyday words, writing in a natural style that sounds like you.

7. Use lists and bullets where appropriate.

8. Aim for writing that is helpful, polite and warm.

9. Use appropriate headings that will help both you and your reader.

10. Write as though you are speaking.

BUILDING GREAT RELATIONSHIPS ONE MESSAGE AT A TIME

No matter how much we love technology, we must never forget the importance of the human touch.
— Shirley Taylor

NOT SO LONG AGO it was primarily letters, meetings, face-to-face discussions and telephone conversations that had a huge bearing on our relationships with customers and colleagues. Today no one can deny that email, instant messaging, social media and technology in general are having a huge impact on our everyday business life. This is particularly so when it comes to dealing with customers, and isn't everyone in the business of providing customer care? You may liaise with internal customers or external customers — both are important.

If you don't pay good attention to customer care skills in everything you do (and everything you do involves email) you can be sure your customers will take their business somewhere else.

In this chapter we will look specifically at tips and techniques that you can use to build relationships with all your customers, both inside and outside the organisation.

Whether you are a home-based entrepreneur or a corporate tycoon, this chapter will show you how to use email to enhance your relationships with your customers and colleagues.

Seven deadly sins of online communication

Read this list of seven deadly sins of online communication and tick the ones that apply to you. If you tick a few of these items, you need help. This chapter will give you lots of advice on how to develop great relationships online.

- ☐ You think what you say is more important than how you say it.

- ☐ You don't think it's important to present an email message attractively with full sentences and a space between paragraphs.

- ☐ You don't know what is meant by creating a special bond with all customers, whether internal or external.

- ☐ You don't realise that a positive working attitude will prove an enjoyable and satisfying way to work.

- ☐ You think big customers should receive better attention than smaller ones.

☐ You get straight to the point in email messages without including any emotions or feelings.

☐ You don't always answer your email promptly.

Using email to build relationships

Customer care has been through many changes in the last few years. More and more companies are realising that positive action is needed to make customer satisfaction their prime aim. If companies are to fight competition, it is essential to make sure that the quality of their products or services is not just satisfactory, but exceptional.

Customers' expectations have changed a lot in recent years as well. Not only is there increased competition because of product similarity, customers are also much better informed and more willing to pay for value. Add to this the rising demand for improved support and the 'I want everything yesterday' mentality, and it's not difficult to see why attention to customer care is vitally important. Let's look at the perceptions of customer service in the past and how things look today:

Yesterday people wanted:	Today people want:
Best price	Best value
Satisfaction	Expectations to be exceeded
To get the job done	To get the job done promptly
Competence	A real bond, real connections

FAST FACT
If you don't take care of your customers, someone else will!

Creating a real bond

Studies show that it takes just 15 seconds for your customer to judge you when you first meet and greet him or her. During these 15 seconds your customer will decide if they will listen to you, believe you and trust you. More important, these 15 seconds will determine if they will buy from you!

The first impression a customer receives is influenced by three things — your words, your body language and your tone of voice. This pie chart shows clearly that it is your body language that is most important — it's how we say things that people pay more attention to.

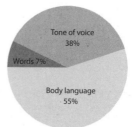

But, I hear you say, in email you don't have the benefit of body language. True. All you have are words and tone, so you have to learn how to use these two aspects to create your own email 'body language'. When you learn to do this, you will be making a real connection — and that's what good customer care is all about.

AHA! MOMENT
It's not what I say that's most important. It's how I say it.

Tips for building great relationships

Your aim must be to create an important connection with all your business contacts — a special bond. This applies whether you are dealing with a person face-to-face, over the telephone, in business meetings or through email.

You can develop great relationships and bonds in email if you remember these tips:

- **Use the customer's name.** Everyone likes to hear their name, so use it. Begin your messages with a greeting and finish off with your name.

- **Avoid jargon.** If you must use words that the customer may not understand, be ready to explain.

- **Be friendly.** You don't want to come across as apathetic. Smile and show warmth — it will make a difference.

- **Be confident and competent.** You must come over as knowledgeable instead of hesitant or unsure. Don't beat about the bush in your email. Be clear and courteous.

- **Show empathy.** This is not the same as sympathy. You must show that you appreciate the other person's point of view or their problems, and that you have a clear understanding of their feelings.

Fast Fact

It is easy to get a customer once. The challenge is keeping the customer. You can keep customers by creating partnerships, by creating bonds. Effective business writing will help.

MYTH BUSTER

I should give my bigger customers better treatment than my not-so-big ones.

Who knows who will become your best customer tomorrow? The one you didn't give a lot of attention today may well be the one who was planning to spend a lot of money with you tomorrow.

AHA! MOMENT

Yes, I can put a smile in my email messages too! Why should you try to do all this when you can get your job done just the same if you just go through the motions? Well, if you try to give a little extra in your day-to-day work, your contacts will feel better and you will feel better too. These principles are not only good for business, but they prove an enjoyable and satisfying way to work.

Let readers hear your voice

With email, you can't see the sender, so you can't read any clues that may help you to interpret the message, e.g. body language, facial expressions, tone of voice, gestures. It's no wonder that so many people misunderstand or misinterpret what is written.

Many people have a friendly conversation with someone on the phone, and then write an email in an unnatural style, using words they would never use in speaking. Compare these two email messages and decide which one you think sounds like Mary's natural voice, her speaking voice, and which one sounds unnatural and forced.

Message 1

Subject: Re: Problem solved

Dear John — We spoke this morning, and note your problem is solved. If you require any further assistance please revert.

Thanks & Regards

Mary Tan

Message 2

Subject: Re: Problem solved

Hi John

Thanks for your call today.

I'm so pleased we've been able to find a solution to this. Good luck with future progress on this project.

I'll be here when you decide how we can help you again.

Mary

FAST FACT

Email should be used to help you build relationships, not break them. Don't undo all your good work on the phone by emailing in a different or unnatural style. In email, you only have words and tone, so you must learn how to use them to create your own email 'body language'. When you learn to do this, you will be making a real connection — and that's what good customer relationships are all about.

MYTH BUSTER

When writing to someone for the first time, I should use very formal language.

Why? Since you are not meeting face-to-face, you cannot offer a hearty handshake, a warm smile of welcome, or show your intense interest with your eyes or posture. While it is not easy, you must try very hard to get something of this in every message you send, particularly when writing to someone new.

Let your readers sense your smile

When you're dealing with people face-to-face, it's often easier than over the telephone or through email because you're dealing with a real person you can hear and see. Even on the telephone, when we can't see the person, you can still hear them and the tone of voice used — and yes, you can hear a smile in a voice. On email you don't have either of these advantages, so you have to take other steps to try to let your readers sense your smile. Some techniques you can use are:

1. Lead your reader into the message

Try not to just dive into a message blindly. Ease the reader into the message by backtracking or giving some basic background information. Be warm and friendly where appropriate. For example:

✓ Thanks for lunch last week. It was great to learn more about your new project, which sounds very interesting.

✓ Thanks for calling me today. It made a nice change to speak to a real person for a change instead of always dealing through email!

✓ I am glad we were able to speak on the telephone this morning. It was good to clarify this issue.

✓ Your news today is interesting. It sounds like you've been working really hard to ensure the success of this project.

2. Show some emotion

Some people give the mere facts and only the facts. They are so keen to get straight to the point that they forget to include any emotions, any feelings. Try to remember that emotive and sensory words add texture and dimension to the general message of what is being written.

You owe it to customers and colleagues to show empathy through your email, using language that will help you in forming a better bond. For example:

✓ I'll be pleased to help you sort out this problem.

✓ I appreciate your understanding in trying to resolve this issue.

✓ I see what you mean and can appreciate your concern.

✓ This has given me a clearer perspective, and I can see a true picture now.

✓ I'm happy to offer you an extra discount of 5% in the circumstances.

Danger Zone

Don't add so much emotion that you come over as gushy. You only need a few extra words to add something to your message and show some warmth.

---

3. Use visual language

Try to paint a picture of what you are communicating. The reader will then be able to see the image that you are trying to create. Use phrases like:

✓ I can see what you mean.

✓ This is all very clear to me now.

✓ This will now enable us to focus on our mutual goals.

✓ Your suggestions look good.

✓ I would like to take a look at this issue from another perspective.

Why should you care what people think?

I'm often told that some people don't care what others think of them based on their emails. They feel that it's not important, as long as the message gets across. Really? Do you really not care if you give a poor impression? Think about it. In the morning when you get up, ask yourself why you take a shower, put on your nicely pressed clothes, fix your hair and make-up? Are you doing this because of what others may think of you if you don't? Not necessarily, right? You're doing it because you care about how you look.

When you write an email in capital letters, filled with abbreviations, typos and grammatical errors, what do you expect the reader to think? When you forward emails with no comment and no thought as to what the recipient may think, how does that make you look? Believe me, people who don't know you will form an immediate impression about your standards and the sort of person you are — and it won't be a good one! They will wonder why you don't seem to care about how others view you. Those who know you well will probably shrug their shoulders and wonder why you can't be bothered to make a simple effort to show some courtesy and make a difference.

FAST FACT

Perception is the only reality in email. It's your choice whether you want to be perceived as educated and courteous. If you simply don't care, then that will be obvious too!

Remember, impressions are important, and you can control what they will be. All you have to do is understand the basic rules of email etiquette and make a tiny bit of effort to display courtesy, consideration and common sense. It won't hurt, and believe me, the benefits are many.

When you are attending a meeting or visiting a client, you always make sure you are suitably dressed. When choosing the packaging for your new product, you always make sure it looks attractive and appealing. Similarly, you must present yourself appropriately online too. Does your email look good? Have you checked to make sure there are no spelling errors? What's the first impression a new customer will receive from your email message?

TRY THIS

Take a look at some of the emails you have sent recently. Consider how they could be improved to help you build better relationships with your readers.

Email can affect careers

I was speaking to a Human Resource colleague recently and she told me that some of her staff are often rude and impulsive in their emails. They prefer to 'shoot out email' rather than discuss things face-to-face.

This may not only affect workplace relationships, but it can also affect careers. Some employees seem to think they can vent their anger on the spot by hitting the 'Send' key, and this can easily erupt into an email war. What we must remember is that an email sent out in haste can come back to haunt you. Apart from the possibility of landing you in court, it lowers productivity, and will almost never get the desired results. It's also not good for morale and job satisfaction.

Building relationships, whether online or offline, involves constant contact throughout the process. If you are to develop successful relationships, you need to learn about your customers' wants and needs at each step, and then personalise each message so that it reflects the relationship you're building with that individual.

Myth Buster

It's only email. Surely it doesn't matter what it sounds like, if I've made a spelling error, or even if it doesn't read quite right.

Wrong. If you don't feel that the spelling, the sound and the look of your email are important, then you are saying that how you present yourself to customers and colleagues is also not important. The opposite is true. How your messages come across to other people has a great impact on readers' perceptions of you, as well as reflecting your communication skills and your professionalism.

STAR TIPS
for building great relationships
one message at a time

1. Remember that how you say something is much more important than what you actually say.

2. Display your messages attractively, using full sentences and with a space between paragraphs.

3. Aim to create a special bond with all your customers — both external and internal.

4. Write in a way that readers hear your voice in every message.

5. Include feelings and emotions in your messages to add a personal touch.

6. Use the same style for writing as you do when speaking.

7. Let readers sense your smile in your messages.

8. Use names to be warm, friendly, and show empathy.

9. Use email as a tool to enhance communication rather than as a replacement for communication.

10. Personalise your messages so people get to know you, and this will help to build relationships.

TOUCHING UP YOUR TONE

Nothing gets in the way of doing business more than language that is anything other than conversational.
— Granville N. Toogood

TONE REFERS TO the attitude you express in the way you deliver a message in either speech or writing. Just like in a conversation, the tone you use in your writing affects the way a reader will interpret and respond to your message.

Of course with email we can't see the writer, so we can't read any clues that may help us to interpret the message, e.g. tone of voice, gestures, body language. Therefore, with written messages there is a great potential for misunderstanding and misinterpretation.

Writing with the wrong tone could damage relationships, and you will not achieve the results you want. Using the right tone will help you to build relationships, influence readers, create a positive impression and get readers to take action.

So, if you're ready to start working on your tone, you're in the right place. Let's get started.

Seven deadly sins of email tone

Read this list of seven deadly sins of email tone and tick the ones that apply to you. If you tick a few of these items, you need help. This chapter will give you lots of advice on how to develop great tone in writing emails.

- ☐ You use a lot of abbreviations even in emails with external customers and people you don't know well.

- ☐ You write a message from your own point of view without thinking about your reader.

- ☐ You have sometimes written a message in anger and later regretted doing so.

- ☐ You use standard template phrases like 'As per', 'Please find' and 'above-mentioned' because everyone else does.

- ☐ You think there should be one way of communicating for writing and a different one for speaking.

- ☐ You have lots of templates that you copy and paste into your emails.

- ☐ You never read your messages out loud before you hit 'Send'.

When speaking to someone face-to-face, it's easy to alter your tone of voice to convey messages in different ways. Much of what you say is also interpreted through non-verbal clues — eye contact, gestures, voice intonation, etc. This is not possible with the written word, so good business writers learn to choose their words very carefully. It is so important to get the tone right, because using the wrong tone could cause real offence to your reader and could lose you an important business contact or friend.

How readers could misinterpret tone

Just because you write in a certain way, it doesn't mean that your reader will receive your message in the same way.

I've read lots of statistics about email and tone. In fact I saw a tweet as I was putting this chapter together saying that over 50 per cent of people interpret the tone of emails incorrectly. That's pretty scary!

Let's try interpreting the email tone in some sample messages:

Message 1
What was written:

> If you don't get this to me by 2 pm today, you won't get your goods on time.

The reader's interpretation:

> It's your own (stupid) fault if you don't get the goods on time.

What could have been written:

> We really want to deliver your goods on schedule. To do this, we need your feedback by 2 pm. Thanks for your help.

Yes, sometimes it might take a few extra words to craft your messages carefully to avoid misunderstanding. Believe me, it's worth it to avoid the confusion and the potential conflict.

Message 2

What was written:

> You said your cheque was mailed on 14 June but it has still not arrived. Please pay my invoice immediately. If it turns up eventually, I'll destroy it.

The reader's interpretation:

> I don't believe you even mailed my cheque. Pay up now, or else!

What could have been written:

> Unfortunately, we have still not received your cheque. I hope you will agree to send another cheque immediately. If the original does arrive, I will of course tear it up.

Read that out loud and you'll see again just how good the tone sounds.

 ### AHA! MOMENT
If we are to achieve our objectives and get the right results from our emails, we need to pay real attention to much more than the words we use.

Right or wrong tone — what happens?

Let's look at what could happen when you use the wrong tone, and what could happen if you use the right tone:

Using the wrong tone will:	Using the right tone will:
Cause misunderstanding	Get your message across clearly
Create conflict	Influence and persuade readers
Make a poor impression	Make a great impression
Damage relationships	Build great relationships
Not get the desired results	Get readers to take action

Just because emails are sent and received quickly, it doesn't mean you should write them quickly and then hit 'Send'. Remember, tone in written language is like body language and facial expressions in person. It goes well beyond grammar and words. Tone projects attitude.

Irritating expressions to avoid

Tone can help to make a message sound firm or friendly, helpful or condescending, according to the impression you wish to convey. Here are some irritating expressions that you should avoid in your writing:

Consider the way these expressions come across, and study the better way:

✗ We cannot do anything about your problem. Try calling an electrician. (abrupt)

✓ **I am sorry that we cannot help with this. I believe an electrician would be better able to help with this type of work.**

✗ Your interview will be held on Wednesday 28 August at 1400 hours. (bossy and unfeeling)

✓ **I hope you can attend an interview on Wednesday 28 August at 2 pm.**

✗ Your computer's guarantee has expired, so you will have to pay for it to be repaired. (blunt)

✓ **The guarantee for your computer has expired, so unfortunately there will be a charge for this.**

✗ Problems of this type are quite common with the cheaper model. Next time I suggest you spend a bit more money. (condescending)

✓ **Problems of this type are far less common with the more advanced model.**

✗ Our phone bills are enormously high. Please stop making so many personal calls. (emotive and sharp)

✓ **The company's telephone bills have increased considerably. Please help by avoiding non-urgent personal calls.**

DANGER ZONE

If you write a message in anger, avoid the temptation of hitting 'Send' straight away. Instead, leave it in your 'Drafts' folder for at least an hour. Go make a cup of coffee, do a few other jobs, do some deep breathing if necessary, then go back and look at your email again. Chances are, you will want to tone it down a bit!

FAST FACT

Instinctively, most people adjust the way they speak depending on their relationship with the person they are addressing. It's important to do this in your business writing too.

Practise your positivity

You can often improve the tone of your messages by using positive words and positive phrases. Positive writing will give the reader a better impression, and will ultimately achieve better results.

Take a look at these three sentences and consider the differences in meaning. Which sentence do you think sounds most positive?

a) We can do this in 3 days.

b) We can do this, but it will take 3 days.

c) We can only get this done in 3 days.

Did you say (a)? Yes, of course this is the most positive. It sounds like you can do it quickly.

If you said (b), you're half right. 'We can do this' is positive. It's the word 'but' that makes the rest of the sentence not so positive. It makes it seem like 3 days is a long time.

I'd be surprised if you said (c). The word 'only' turns this sentence into a negative, and it sounds like 3 days is a long time.

FAST FACT

Negative language triggers negative results. Use positive words like these in your writing: results, guarantee, benefit, preferred, recommended, time-saving, safe, fast, proven, can, will.

Read these negative sentences carefully and then study how they can be written more positively:

✗ Have your report on my desk by 8 am tomorrow at the latest.
✓ **Please let me have your report by 8 am tomorrow morning.**

✗ You neglected to report these serious errors early enough.
✓ **It is unfortunate that you did not report these errors earlier.**

✗ I have looked through your report and am totally confused. Please see me urgently to clarify.
✓ **I have several questions about your report. Let's meet soon to discuss this.**

✗ This model is very popular but it only does 35 miles to the litre.

✓ **This model is very popular and it does about 35 miles to the litre.**

✗ If you do not return your form before 1 August you will be too late to attend the conference.

✓ **Please return your form by 31 July so that we can register your name for the conference.**

✗ I regret to inform you that the alterations will not be finished until next week.

✓ **The alterations will be finished next Friday.**

 DANGER ZONE
Be very obvious with your meanings in email, since subtleties can often be lost or completely misunderstood. Remember this too when reading other people's email. Their understanding of the language, or their haste in composing the email, may have given it a 'tone' that can easily come across as being derogatory or aggressive. Reread it and see if you are simply misinterpreting the words.

Keep it courteous while keeping it brief

Many people ask for advice about how to keep their messages short and to the point without coming across as being abrupt and cold. Of course, courtesy is important, and it can be achieved with care and thought. Let's take a look at a few examples of how some messages could be improved while retaining clarity. Notice how all the improved versions are so much more personal and warm too:

✗ Please find below the best available rate at The Westin Sydney.

✓ **Here are our best available rates at The Westin Sydney.**

✗ Kindly see attached on my department's performance for last month.

✓ **Here is my performance report for March 2017.**

✗ Your immediate feedback will be highly appreciated so we can advise the guest accordingly.

✓ **Please let me have your urgent feedback so we can let the guest know.**

✗ Kindly revert back with flight schedule upon confirmation and also with names of delegates, and liaise accordingly with our Martin Lim upon arrival at airport for transportation and hotel arrangements.

✓ **Please let me know the delegates' names and their flight schedule. They should liaise with Martin Lim when they arrive regarding hotel arrangements.**

✗ With regards your enquiry on the distance from the Langkawi Orchid Hotel to the Langkawi Golf & Spa Resort. It is very close, around 5 minutes by taxi.

✓ **Many thanks for your call. The Langkawi Orchid Hotel is just five minutes away from the Langkawi Golf & Spa Resort by taxi.**

✗ As spoken earlier with regards to your quotation ref xxxxx, pls advise whether possible for your goodself to come down to our company on 11 June (Wed) at 9.30 am for a short discussion with my senior technical manager on this issue.

✓ **Thanks for your call today. It would be helpful if you could attend a short meeting with my senior technical manager. Is 9.30 am on Wednesday 11 June good for you?**

✗ As per our telephone conversation, kindly find attached a copy of the credit card authorisation form.

✓ **Thank you for your call. Attached is a copy of our credit card authorisation form.**

✗ Please revert with your agreement to enable us to adjust the points on your account accordingly.

✓ **We will be happy to adjust the points as soon as we receive your agreement.**

✗ Anticipating your soonest reply.

✓ **I look forward to your reply.**

FAST FACT

'Revert' does not mean 'reply'. It means to relapse or regress, to go back to a former condition. So please don't write, 'Please revert to me.'

Is your writing warm or cold?

Being courteous and businesslike should not mean cold. However, very often writers today use language that doesn't sound like a human being — language that's distant, formal, stuffy and cold. Let's look at some examples of cold messages that need warming up:

Cold	Warm
We refer to your letter of 12 June.	Thank you for your letter of 12 June.
We thank you in advance for your kind cooperation.	Thank you for your help.
Kindly find attached my monthly performance report for Marketing Department.	Here is my department's performance report for March.
Please find below best available rates at The Westin Sydney.	I'm pleased to give you our best available rates at The Westin Sydney.
Please find attached our latest catalogue for your reference.	I'm attaching our latest catalogue, and I hope you find it interesting.
Appreciate if you could provide us with the above information together with a contact number to reach you.	Please let me have this information soon together with your telephone number.

In each of the warm examples, you will note that they are friendly and conversational too, while getting straight to the point. You can almost imagine yourself saying these sentences if you were speaking.

 Aha! Moment
I need to read sentences out loud and imagine I'm speaking to the reader. This will help me make sure I'm writing in a conversational style.

Another example of positive/negative tone

My friend recently told me that she emailed two insurance agents with the same enquiry. Based on their replies, which one would you prefer to work with?

Agent A's reply

> Hi Marianna
>
> We have received your email. As you are over 30, you will need to pay a premium of $3000 per year. Kindly let me know when I can visit you to introduce our policies.

Agent B's reply

> Hi Marianna
>
> I'd be happy to discuss your insurance needs. As you are under 40, you are eligible for a premium of $3000 per year. Please let me know when it's convenient and I'll be pleased to drop by and introduce our policies.

Last word on tone

In all business messages, you should aim for an overall tone that is:

- **Confident:** Confidence conveys authority and creates trust. It also assures the reader that you are competent.

- **Conversational:** When you write in a natural style, similar to how you speak, you'll develop better relationships. Avoid using the stilted, highly formal wording used in the past, with lots of redundancies and jargon.

- **Courteous:** Aim to be polite and respectful. Avoid lecturing the reader, or using language that suggests the reader is at fault or unreasonable. It's very important that what you write will not offend the reader.

- **Positive:** Always look for helpful and encouraging ways to put across a message wherever possible. Avoid negatives unless essential, and focus on benefits and strengths.

STAR TIPS
for touching up your tone

1. Compose emails with the reader in mind.

2. Avoid template phrases like 'As per' and 'Please find'.

3. Use positive instead of negative language.

4. Keep your messages courteous and at the same time keep them brief.

5. Use language that sounds like a human being, not a boring template.

6. Read messages out loud before sending, and consider how they sound.

7. Aim for a conversational, natural tone that sounds like your own speaking voice.

8. Use warm, natural, friendly tone instead of cold, formal and unnatural.

9. Don't write an email in anger, as it could come back to haunt you.

10. Use the right tone and you will build great relationships and get great results.

PLANNING AND STRUCTURING YOUR MESSAGES

Plan your work for today and every day, then work your plan.

— Norman Vincent Peale

ANY WRITING is best tackled systematically, using an approach with a logical flow. There are many things you need to think about before you even start putting your fingers on the keyboard. And when you've finished the document, you must not hit 'Send' until you are quite sure it's all good to go.

A well-structured document written in good business language is the key to effective communication. This chapter will help you to get past that blank page and start creating well-structured documents that will get the right results.

Seven deadly sins of planning and structuring your messages

Read this list of seven deadly sins and tick the ones that apply to you. If you tick a few of these items, you need help. This chapter will provide all the guidance you need.

- ☐ You sometimes don't know where to start a message, and your fingers sit on the keyboard for ages wondering how to begin.

- ☐ You get straight to the point in some email messages, without considering an appropriate opening to lead in nicely.

- ☐ You jump back and forth between topics instead of arranging them logically to help your reader.

- ☐ You think it's acceptable to write your entire message in one paragraph.

- ☐ Your recipients sometimes write back asking you to clarify certain points from your email.

- ☐ You don't think it's important to reflect for a moment before you begin an email to ask yourself what's the purpose of your message.

- ☐ You don't organise your thoughts before you start writing, and then you wonder why writing is so difficult.

Seven steps to success in planning messages

Here's a formula that will help you to PRODUCE first-class email messages:

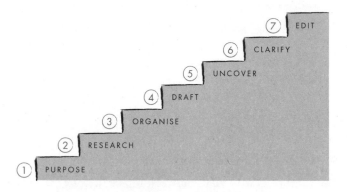

Step 1: Purpose
Ask yourself lots of questions before you start writing:

- Why am I writing this message?

- What do I want to achieve?

- What are my objectives?

- How will I get the right results?

Step 2: Research
You wouldn't start baking a cake unless you had all the ingredients, would you? So it is with writing. Gather all the information together that will help you get your message across. Ask yourself:

- What does the reader know already?

- What will help the reader to understand?

- What important details do I need to give?

- What will the reader's attitude be?

Step 3: Organise

Here is where you need to sort your ideas out in a logical order. I will be discussing my Four-Point Plan with you soon, which will help you structure your messages in a very systematic way.

Step 4: Draft

Now you are ready to put your fingers on the keyboard and draft your message, remembering all the points discussed in the previous chapters of course.

DANGER ZONE

This is the point at which may people hit 'Send'! It will never be the right thing to do, and may be a big mistake. Don't hit 'Send' until you have satisfied yourself that you have gone through all seven steps in this model.

Step 5: Uncover the reader's reaction

This is probably the most important step. It's where you take off your head and put on the head of the reader. Ask yourself:

- Are all the facts and figures correct?

- Have I missed anything out, or included anything irrelevant?

- Will the reader understand everything, or will clarification be necessary?

- Is the action stated clearly?

- Is the message clear, concise, courteous and complete?

Step 6: Clarify

If you are not completely happy with your draft, you must make some changes to clarify your message. Improve the structure, the tone, the choice of words. Keep the reader and your objectives in mind.

Step 7: Edit

Once again, go through your document with a fine-tooth comb. Check for grammar, spelling, and punctuation, and then check again.

AHA! MOMENT

Once I get into the habit of going through this seven-step process, it will become automatic and like second nature to me. I will reap the rewards.

The Four-Point Plan for structuring messages logically

Many email messages are short and routine. They can often be written without any special preparation. However, others may take more thought and planning.

When I ask people what goes wrong in emails, one of the most common complaints is that they find it difficult to focus when reading a message that's all jumbled up and badly structured. Busy business people don't want to have to hunt all over the place for the most important details in an email message. They need everything written in a logical order, with the action stated clearly and simply.

I've been teaching this Four-Point Plan for many years, and I'm confident that it's one of the keys to writing effectively. Let's take a quick look at each of the four sections of this Four-Point Plan, and then we'll look in more detail at each section:

1. Opening	Think of this as the background and basics. This is where you set the scene. You may refer to a telephone conversation, an email, a meeting, an enquiry.	Keep this section short. Just set the scene.
2. Details	Think of this as all the facts and figures. Give all the information (or ask for it). Provide all relevant details. Use short paragraphs with a space between each.	The longest section of your message. Make sure it flows logically.

3. Action	This is where you tell the reader the response you want. You may sometimes begin here with a conclusion.	What do you want the reader to do next?
4. Closing	Usually a simple one-line sentence to finish off.	Make it relevant.

Openings

The opening section of an email seems to be one that causes the most difficulty for writers. People tell me they put their fingers on the keyboard and often don't know where to start. As a result, openings can often become very stilted and artificial. Remember, it's here you want to create a real bond with your reader, so use friendly, modern sentences instead of the wooden and unnatural phrases that we see so often:

Instead of:	**Write:**
As spoken...	**Thanks for your call this morning.**
We spoke.	**It was great to speak to you.**
We received your message.	**Thanks for your message.** **Thank you for your email.** **It was good to hear from you today.**

Instead of:	Write:
This follows our meeting earlier.	**It was good to meet you this morning.** **Thank you for your time this morning.**
Your order was received today.	**Many thanks for your order.**
We are organising a conference for leaders on 12 November 2017.	**STTS Training is proud to invite you to our exciting leadership conference in November.**

 ### Try This

If you are often stuck on how to begin your emails, think about your aim. Is it to:

- Alert a manager to a problem?
- Request details and information?
- Notify someone about a meeting?
- Persuade a manager to increase your budget?

Mention this key point in the first paragraph and it should then be easier to elaborate with all the essential details.

Details

This will be the central and longest part of your message. Think of it as the meat in your sandwich. It is where you give all the new information, or reply to the reader's queries. This is where you will include the facts and figures, giving all the information the reader needs. Remember to separate this section into paragraphs where appropriate, with one line space between each. You may have to restructure this part before you finalise your message, so that you ensure all the details flow nicely in a logical order.

Action

This section may begin with a conclusion. For example, in a letter of complaint you may begin this section with 'I am very disappointed with the way I was treated'. You will then proceed by stating what action you expect the reader to take, or what you will do next, for example:

✓ I hope you will investigate this situation and take the necessary action.

✓ Please complete the attached reply form and return it to me by 12 July.

✓ Please let me have your report by next Monday 21 October.

✓ Our Customer Service Manager, Mr James Tan, will contact you soon to arrange an appointment to meet you.

Closings

You can often ruin an email with a boring close, so always make sure you finish off with something relevant and thoughtful.

Instead of:	Write:
Please revert to me at your soonest.	I hope to hear from you soon.
Your prompt reply would be appreciated.	I look forward to your prompt reply.

Instead of:	Write:
Please do not hesitate to contact me should you require any further information.	**Please call me if you have any questions.**
Please feel free to contact me if you need further assistance.	**Please let me know if you need any help.**

A final word about closings

I just don't get it. A close like 'Thank you and Regards' does nothing for me. It just tells me the writer has given no thought to putting his personality into the message and just wants to be like all his colleagues and not stand out at all.

If you have been courteous throughout your message (and no matter what the circumstances, you must always be courteous) there should be no need to finish every email with 'Thank you' or, worse still, 'Thank you and Regards'. Thank you for what? Thank you for reading my message?

Think of something more proactive to close with. For example:

✓ Thanks for your help.

✓ Thanks for your patience.

✓ Thanks for your understanding.

✓ Thank you for your support.

Personally, I have never used 'Regards' and I never will. I find it boring, unfeeling and unnecessary. Why not make up your own personal close, or don't use a close at all? For example:

- If you know you're going to see me next week:

    See you soon.

- If you want a reply from me:

    Hope to hear from you soon.

- If someone has been helpful and has given you what you need:

    Thanks for your help.

- It's Friday:

    Have a great weekend.

 MYTH BUSTER

We should always finish our messages with 'Thank you'.

Thank you for what? For reading the message? Forget it. If you have been courteous in your message, no one will ever miss a boring 'Thank you' at the end. So drop it, unless you say thank you for something, for example:

- Thank you for your help.
- Thank you for your patience.
- Thanks for your understanding.
- Thanks for all your support.

The Four-Point Plan in practice

Study these examples of well-structured emails:

Example 1

> To: lilytan@healthylife.com
>
> Subject: Re: Eating for Health campaign
>
> Hi Lily
>
> Thanks for your message. I'm excited to hear about your 'Eating for Health' campaign next month.
>
> I'm delighted to accept your invitation to give the opening address at the launch on 15 November. I think it would be valuable if we could meet to discuss how I should focus my opening, and key points you want me to mention. I want to make sure I address all the objectives of your campaign.
>
> Please let me know if 11 am next Tuesday 7 October is convenient for you. I could meet you at your office, or you are welcome to come over here to mine. Please let me have your draft programme before our meeting.
>
> I look forward to hearing from you, and participating in this exciting campaign.
>
> Martin Fong
> General Manager
> Orchid Superstores
> Tel: +65 68287722
> Mobile: +65 82394920

Use an appropriate greeting.

The opening refers to the email and sets the scene.

Include all relevant details using a friendly, conversational tone.

Action is specified clearly and logically.

A nice relevant close helps to create rapport and build bonds.

I don't see why we need 'Regards'. Just relevant contact details.

Example 2

To: limbeeleng@orchid.com.my

Subject: Customer Service

Dear Mrs Lim

The opening in this complaint pays a compliment by referring to previous good service.

I have been a customer of Orchid Departmental Store for the past 10 years, and have usually been very pleased with the service I have received.

The word 'However' introduces a contrast to the picture painted in the opening.

Full details of the incident are given in a straightforward, clear style, stating all the facts.

However, when I visited your Ladieswear Department on Monday 17 October, one of your assistants, Sandra Wong, was very unprofessional. She continued talking to her colleague after I asked for some help. When I persisted, she eventually snapped 'You'll have to be quick — I'm due for my break soon'.

The writer forms a conclusion first, and then states the action he wants the reader to take.

This is not the type of service I am used to receiving at your store, and I was most surprised and offended by her reaction. I do hope you will investigate this and review your customer service policy with this assistant.

An appropriate closing is used.

I look forward to a prompt reply.

Jonathan Leng
Mobile: +65 81868588

Using lists and bullets

Lists can be very useful in our writing. Lists are great because they help you to:

- Organise your thoughts and your points

- Guide your reader's attention to key points

- Simplify detailed or complicated topics

- Make it easier for readers to scan or skim

- Enhance visual impact

Make sure, however, that your list items are parallel in structure. In this example, every point in this list needs to follow '…they help you to:' in the lead sentence, so using a verb at the beginning of each point works well.

FAST FACT
When you need to write a list of procedures or instructions for people to follow, it's a great idea to start each point with a verb (action word). So many people start each point with 'To…', which is completely unnecessary.

Here's an alternative style. Remember that every bullet must follow this lead sentence, so using a verb will not work this time. Here we need to be consistent in starting with words ending in 'ing'.

You can improve your business writing by:

- Adopting a friendly, conversational writing style

- Organising your points carefully and logically

- Reading your message out loud to check the tone

- Keeping to the point and staying focused

- Using language that the reader will understand

Numbers or bullets?

Numbered lists are useful when the sequence or order of the information is important. The numbers may also create a frame of reference even when the particular order may not be important. You can use numbered lists when you are:

- Listing steps, instructions or rules

- Showing that the order of the list matters

- Referring to the list items later in the document

Here are two more email messages with notes about the structure:

Example 3

To: liz.cheong@sttstraining.com

Subject: Customer Service Training

Hi Liz

It was good to speak to you today about the two-day workshop we are hoping to organise for our staff.

> A friendly opening, referring to the telephone conversation.

There will be 15 staff for this training, ranging in service from 6 months to 5 years. We would like the workshop to include:

> A friendly, conversational style will help to build bonds.

> All relevant details are given.

- understanding the nature of conflict
- creating and maintaining a service culture
- managing customers' expectations
- dealing with difficult situations
- repairing relationships with customers
- writing effective emails to customers

> All points are written in the same grammatical style.

Please let me have your proposal, including a detailed outline and profiles of your trainers, plus your professional fees.

> The action is stated clearly.

I hope to hear from you soon.

> A nice close finishes off the message.

Lee Fong

Ong Lee Fong
Training Director
RBF Services Pte Ltd
Tel: +65 6343242
www.rbfservices.com

> This signature gives all contact details.

Example 4

To: limleefong@rbfservices.com

Subject: Re: Customer Service Training

Hi Lee Fong

The opening refers to the call and email.

Thanks for your call and email today.

A friendly, conversational style is used.

I am very pleased you thought of us for this Customer Service Training programme. I will put a proposal together for you and send this to you tomorrow morning.

Action is clearly stated.

All the relevant details are included.

I suggest we should meet to discuss this in more detail so we can ensure our programme is customised to your specific requirements. Can I suggest next Friday 19 August at 2.30 pm at our offices?

A friendly, appropriate closing is used.

I am looking forward to working with you on this.

Liz

Liz Cheong
Senior Consultant
STTS Training Pte Ltd
www.sttstraining.com
Tel: +65 95535670

DANGER ZONE

Beware writing a list of points that are not grammatically parallel, as it could confuse your reader. If you start one point with a verb, make sure that all points start with a verb.

Using headings with bullets

One big complaint about writing is when paragraphs get very lengthy and drag on and on so the message becomes very long and complicated. Without any proper structure, it is easy to lose focus. In these cases, it's always a good idea to consider how you could use headings to break the material into different sections, and perhaps also bullets to list details.

Here is an example of an email that is very poorly written and badly formatted. You can see how difficult it would be for the reader to pick out the key points:

Subject: Unauthorised parking

Dear all

Please be informed that the company's new car parking arrangements will come into effect in two week's time.

Appreciate your co-operation with the new rules to ensure there is no unauthorised parking, this would cause great inconvenience to the large lorries that deliver raw materials to our factory.

A parking plan is attached herewith for your reference and perusal. All staff are instructed to park only in the areas indicated on the plan specially for staff and they should display their red permit on their car windscreen, these permits can be obtained from security gate. As for visitors, they will be given green permits when they report to the security gate, please note that special areas have been reserve for visitors as indicated on the above plan. All staff must inform security gate when visitors are expected.

For your convenience a copy of the above-mentioned parking plan has also been placed on all company notice board.

Your co-operation is appreciated. Should you require any further information please do not hesitate to contact me for clarifications.

Thank you and regards.

Here is the same email, structured well using the Four-Point Plan, and sectioned off with numbered points, headings and bullets. All the information is very clear and scannable, the reader can find all the key points easily, the bullets are displayed consistently, and it is written in plain English.

Subject: 10 May – New car parking arrangements

Dear Colleagues

I'm pleased to announce that our new car parking arrangements will come into effect on Monday, 10 May.

Please take a look at the attached parking plan showing the special areas for staff and visitors. This plan can also be seen on all company notice boards.

Here are the new procedures for car parking:

Staff
- Collect your red permit from the security gate.
- Display your permit on your car windscreen.
- Park in designated areas for staff.

Visitors
- Inform security when expecting visitors.
- Ask visitors to collect their green permit from the security gate.
- Park in designated areas for visitors.

Thank you for your help in ensuring that these new car parking arrangements are successful.

John Tan
Administration Manager

STAR TIPS
for planning and structuring messages

1. Before beginning any message, ask yourself what is the purpose and what do you want to achieve.

2. Remember to go through the seven-step process, and don't just hit 'Send' after your first attempt.

3. Use the Four-Point Plan consistently to help you structure your messages logically.

4. Begin your message using your own words instead of those of our great-grandfathers.

5. Use a friendly conversational style instead of wooden, unnatural phrases.

6. Help the reader by including an action statement telling them exactly what you expect them to do.

7. Remember grammatical parallelism when compiling lists.

8. Make sure your message looks visually attractive.

9. Read your messages out loud so you can check if you are writing in a natural style.

10. Plan and structure your email messages with care to avoid a lot of ding-dong!

10

SOME FORMULAS AND SAMPLE EMAILS

You can have brilliant ideas, but if you can't get them across, your ideas won't get you anywhere.
— Lee Iacocca

IF YOU'RE LIKE MANY PEOPLE, you often put your fingers on the keyboard and wonder where to start writing a message. I'm not a fan of template writing, but I am a fan of formulas. Formulas can be very useful because they take you step-by-step through the essentials of what to include in a message and where.

In this final chapter, we will focus on some specific formulas and some great sample emails. You'll also learn how formulas can help you with very challenging messages.

The Four-Point Plan

All these formulas are based on the Four-Point Plan that we looked at in Chapter 9, so let's remind ourselves about this here:

1. Opening	Think of this as the background and basics. This is where you set the scene. You may refer to a telephone conversation, an email, a meeting, an enquiry.	Keep this section short. Just set the scene.
2. Details	Think of this as all the facts and figures. Give all the information (or ask for it). Provide all relevant details. Use short paragraphs with a space between each.	The longest section of your message. Make sure it flows logically.
3. Action	This is where you tell the reader the response you want. You may sometimes begin here with a conclusion.	What do you want the reader to do next?
4. Closing	Usually a simple one-line sentence to finish off.	Make it relevant.

Formula 1: Request for information

One of the most common and simple messages to write is when we need to ask for information. In this formula we will write a message to a hotel asking if their ballroom is available for an event.

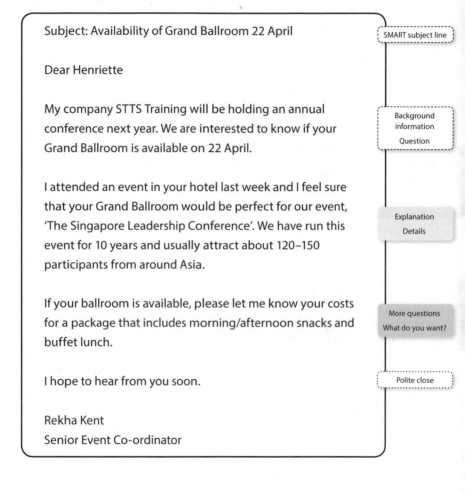

Subject: Availability of Grand Ballroom 22 April

SMART subject line

Dear Henriette

My company STTS Training will be holding an annual conference next year. We are interested to know if your Grand Ballroom is available on 22 April.

Background information
Question

I attended an event in your hotel last week and I feel sure that your Grand Ballroom would be perfect for our event, 'The Singapore Leadership Conference'. We have run this event for 10 years and usually attract about 120–150 participants from around Asia.

Explanation
Details

If your ballroom is available, please let me know your costs for a package that includes morning/afternoon snacks and buffet lunch.

More questions
What do you want?

I hope to hear from you soon.

Polite close

Rekha Kent
Senior Event Co-ordinator

Formula 2: Reply to request for information

It can be so frustrating to have a ding-dong of emails going back and forth with people asking more questions. You can save yourself valuable time by using this simple formula, which will make sure you give all the information the reader needs. We will write a reply here from the hotel that received the email in Formula 1.

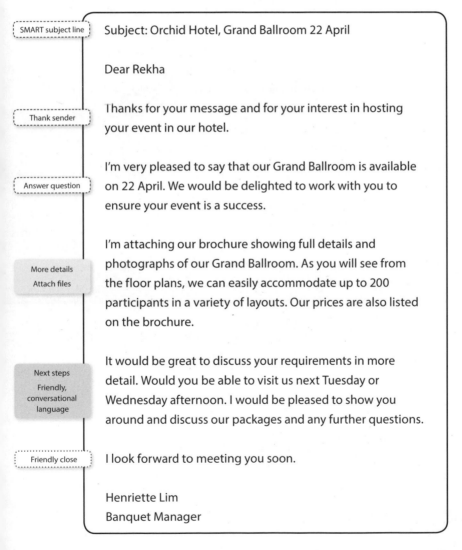

SMART subject line

Subject: Orchid Hotel, Grand Ballroom 22 April

Dear Rekha

Thank sender

Thanks for your message and for your interest in hosting your event in our hotel.

Answer question

I'm very pleased to say that our Grand Ballroom is available on 22 April. We would be delighted to work with you to ensure your event is a success.

More details
Attach files

I'm attaching our brochure showing full details and photographs of our Grand Ballroom. As you will see from the floor plans, we can easily accommodate up to 200 participants in a variety of layouts. Our prices are also listed on the brochure.

Next steps
Friendly, conversational language

It would be great to discuss your requirements in more detail. Would you be able to visit us next Tuesday or Wednesday afternoon. I would be pleased to show you around and discuss our packages and any further questions.

Friendly close

I look forward to meeting you soon.

Henriette Lim
Banquet Manager

Formula 3: Good news message

There are often opportunities to send good news messages in business. Perhaps when someone has been promoted, been awarded a special contract, an award, weddings or births. Such messages are always appreciated and they are very good for business.

In this example, your top sales representative has won a special award. You decide to write to your clients to let them know this news. All employees feel better when they feel appreciated, so this is great for your colleague and could be great for business.

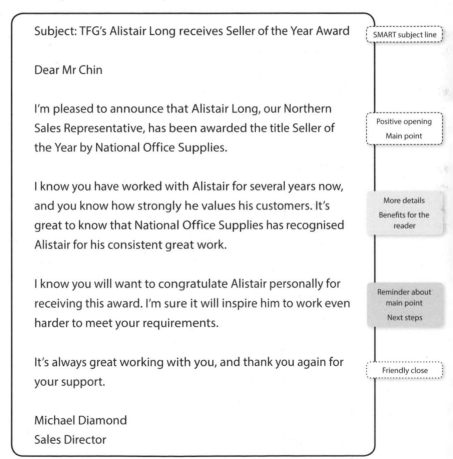

Subject: TFG's Alistair Long receives Seller of the Year Award   *SMART subject line*

Dear Mr Chin

I'm pleased to announce that Alistair Long, our Northern Sales Representative, has been awarded the title Seller of the Year by National Office Supplies.   *Positive opening / Main point*

I know you have worked with Alistair for several years now, and you know how strongly he values his customers. It's great to know that National Office Supplies has recognised Alistair for his consistent great work.   *More details / Benefits for the reader*

I know you will want to congratulate Alistair personally for receiving this award. I'm sure it will inspire him to work even harder to meet your requirements.   *Reminder about main point / Next steps*

It's always great working with you, and thank you again for your support.   *Friendly close*

Michael Diamond
Sales Director

Formula 4: Bad news message

Of course, delivering bad news or negative information is going to be more challenging than delivering good news. Tone will be very important in this type of message, especially when you know you are likely to disappoint the reader.

In any message of this type, you should have four aims, which are to:

- Deliver the bad news

- Gain acceptance for the bad news

- Maintain the goodwill of the reader

- Reflect a good image of the organisation

In this email we will work on a scenario where a sales director has to write to clients about a price increase. This is inevitable in most businesses, so you need to be very convincing.

Subject: New price lists from XYZ

Dear Don

Background or buffer to soften the blow

Over the past few years, many businesses have been experiencing steadily rising costs. I'm sure you can appreciate that our own costs have continued to rise with this general trend.

Clear, logical reasons for the news or decision

Increasing world demand has been an important factor in raising the prices of our imported raw materials. On top of this, there have been constantly rising overheads.

We have delayed this decision for as long as possible, but unfortunately we have no option but to make changes now. Our new price lists are attached, and they will take effect from 1 October.

Bad news delivered tactfully

We are sorry these increases are necessary. However, they amount to an average of only about 5%, and we hope you will agree that these are not unreasonable.

Apologise

Positive close

Thank you again for your support.

Alan Rushton
Senior Sales Director

Formula 5: Making a complaint

There are bound to be occasions in business when it's necessary to make a complaint. Effective complaints are concise, authoritative, factual, constructive and friendly. In this scenario we are writing to a popular grocery store to complain about a recent purchase.

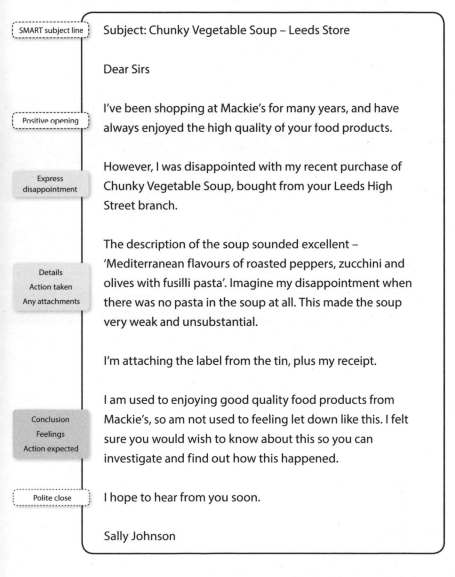

SMART subject line — Subject: Chunky Vegetable Soup – Leeds Store

Dear Sirs

Positive opening — I've been shopping at Mackie's for many years, and have always enjoyed the high quality of your food products.

Express disappointment — However, I was disappointed with my recent purchase of Chunky Vegetable Soup, bought from your Leeds High Street branch.

Details / Action taken / Any attachments — The description of the soup sounded excellent – 'Mediterranean flavours of roasted peppers, zucchini and olives with fusilli pasta'. Imagine my disappointment when there was no pasta in the soup at all. This made the soup very weak and unsubstantial.

I'm attaching the label from the tin, plus my receipt.

Conclusion / Feelings / Action expected — I am used to enjoying good quality food products from Mackie's, so am not used to feeling let down like this. I felt sure you would wish to know about this so you can investigate and find out how this happened.

Polite close — I hope to hear from you soon.

Sally Johnson

Formula 6: Replying to a complaint

Most organisations want to hear from customers who are unhappy. It provides them with an opportunity to investigate, explain and put things right. Your reply to any complaint should be professional, friendly and aimed at regaining customer goodwill.

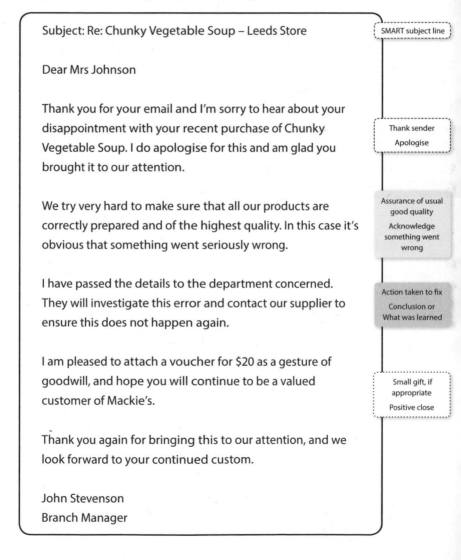

Subject: Re: Chunky Vegetable Soup – Leeds Store

SMART subject line

Dear Mrs Johnson

Thank you for your email and I'm sorry to hear about your disappointment with your recent purchase of Chunky Vegetable Soup. I do apologise for this and am glad you brought it to our attention.

Thank sender
Apologise

We try very hard to make sure that all our products are correctly prepared and of the highest quality. In this case it's obvious that something went seriously wrong.

Assurance of usual good quality
Acknowledge something went wrong

I have passed the details to the department concerned. They will investigate this error and contact our supplier to ensure this does not happen again.

Action taken to fix
Conclusion or What was learned

I am pleased to attach a voucher for $20 as a gesture of goodwill, and hope you will continue to be a valued customer of Mackie's.

Small gift, if appropriate
Positive close

Thank you again for bringing this to our attention, and we look forward to your continued custom.

John Stevenson
Branch Manager

Formula 7: Writing reminders

Most people can't remember everything, so reminders are sometimes inevitable. Perhaps a colleague hasn't sent you that report you need. A client hasn't paid your invoice. A manager keeps you waiting for essential information to move ahead with a project.

Situations like this can be very frustrating and challenging. If you deal with them in the wrong way, it can damage a relationship. If you deal with them well, it can promote goodwill.

When you feel rushed and stressed, you may come across as abrupt or harsh in your emails. It will take some effort, but you can write challenging messages in a non-threatening way. Remember to use relationship-building language, not relationship-breaking language.

In this scenario you have asked all your team for information that you need to compile a report for management. The only person who hasn't replied is Mandy. You really need her input urgently.

Let's look first at how not to write this message:

> Mandy
>
> You haven't sent me the details I requested. I need your input by 5pm today.
>
> This is urgent now.
>
> Sally

With no 'Hi' or 'Dear', the opening is not friendly. Using 'you' language here is very blaming, and the blunt nature of the message would put Mandy on the defensive.

Now let's look at a great formula for writing such a challenging message:

Subject: Management report details needed by 5pm today | SMART subject line

Hi Mandy

I know you're busy, and hopefully you're working on this right now. | Give reader the benefit of doubt / Don't make accusations

I just wanted to remind you that I really need your input as mentioned in my emails below. | Reminder about what you need. / Use 'I' not 'You' statements

Please get this to me by 5pm today at the latest. I can then submit my management report on time. | State deadline and reason/consequences

If you have any questions, please call me soon. | Polite, proactive close

Many thanks

Sally

Formula 8: Saying 'no' nicely

When you must say 'no' to someone, it's important to choose your words carefully. It's best not to rush with an email like this. State your 'no' clearly and confidently, using tact and diplomacy. Even though you are saying 'no' to someone, it helps to write with an aim of preserving the relationship.

Here's a scenario. Your boss has asked you to take the lead on a new project launching this year's company-wide fundraiser. You are already beginning to feel overwhelmed with work, and just recently started helping two other department heads with their admin tasks in addition to the workload from your main boss. Plus you recently volunteered to help on the team organising the annual dinner and dance. So now you feel you have to say 'no' to your boss's request.

Let's look first at how not to write this message:

> Dear Michael
>
> I'm writing regarding your recent request for me to take the lead on this new project.
>
> I'm really pushed to my limit right now, so I have to say no to this request. With all the extra work recently for Sandra and Oliver, I don't see how I could possibly take on any more.
>
> If I didn't have so much work on right now, I would have said yes. I enjoy my job but there are only so many hours in a day.
>
> Best regards
>
> Joanna

If you read this message out loud, you will see how harsh it comes across. Starting with 'I'm writing…' is never a good idea. Using language like 'I'm really pushed to the limit' and 'There are only so many hours in a day' is not helpful or tactful. Now let's look at how it should be done:

Subject: Request to lead fundraising project

SMART subject line

Dear Michael

I've given a lot of thought to your request for me to lead the company-wide fundraising project.

Neutral, positive opening

As you know, I've recently taken on extra administration work for Sandra Choo and Oliver Lim, and I am enjoying helping them. However, with your work on top of this, it means that I'm working at my full capacity right now.

Explain why
'Softly softly' approach
Give a clear but tactful 'no'
Use 'I' statements

I love my job, and I'm very keen to do it well, so this is my main priority. While I'm honoured to be asked to take on this new project, I feel I must decline right now. However, when another lead is chosen, I would be very happy to serve on the committee, with the possibility of leading this project next year instead.

Thank and show commitment
Any further steps?

I do hope you will understand my reasoning on this.

Positive, polite close

Thanks again for your support.

Joanna

Formula 9: Follow-up message to potential clients

Writing messages to potential clients is one of the most important marketing tasks. It's an essential step to developing the relationship and moving your connections further up the sales ladder.

Perhaps you've met potential new clients at a trade show, a networking event or a conference. Now you need to help them get to know you a little better. You need to work on helping them to like you and trust you.

So in this scenario we are going to write an email to some clients you have met recently at a conference.

But first let's look at how not to write this message:

> Dear Denise
>
> We met at the San Diego convention last week. I believe you said you wanted to create a new website for your business.
>
> We help clients with all their design needs at reasonable prices, and we can work on anything like logos, websites, brochures and flyers.
>
> Attached please find our brochure giving more details of our services. Kindly refer to our website to see links to some recent projects.
>
> Please contact me soon to arrange to meet to discuss this.
>
> Thanks and regards
>
> Ayesha Abadi

The opening is not confident or upbeat. The second paragraph sounds very salesy and not at all personalised. Language like 'please find' and 'kindly refer' is old-fashioned and unnatural. Overall, it sounds very template-like, and could definitely do with warming up!

Now let's look at how it should be done:

Subject: Great to meet you at Women Leaders Convention

SMART subject line

Dear Denise

It was great to meet you last Tuesday at the Women Leaders Convention in Kuwait. I thoroughly enjoyed our discussion over lunch, and was interested to hear that you want to create a new website for your speaking business.

Personal introduction mentioning where you met
Warm, friendly language

As I mentioned, we specialise in helping clients with all their design needs, including logos, websites, brochures and fliers. Our aim is to create unique designs that reflect who our clients are, at a price they can afford.

Explain what you do
Not too salesy

I'm attaching our brochure giving more details of all our services. You will find links to some of our recent projects on our website.

Extra details or attachments
Conversational language

I'll be in your area next week, and wondered if you have some time on Thursday or Friday to meet me. I'd love to discuss this with you more.

Positive, proactive closing
Warm, emotional language

I hope to hear from you soon.

Ayesha Abadi

Formula 10: Persuasive messages

Very often in business, we have to persuade someone around to our way of thinking, or influence or convince someone about a course of action.

It's important to be diplomatic when writing to persuade or convince. You have to make it sound like your ideas are the only sensible choice, and get them around to your way of thinking. This can be a real challenge, but with careful attention to tone, you can do it.

We're going to look at this scenario here. Your company recently set up a specialised Central Sourcing Department to do all the sourcing and buying for other departments. Unfortunately, one department has sourced its own supplier without involving you. The manager emailed you asking you to approve their supplier's proposal. So you need to write an email reminding them about your department's role and asking them to let you do their sourcing from now on. Keep in mind that you don't want them to feel forced into it — you want them to see that it's in their best interests.

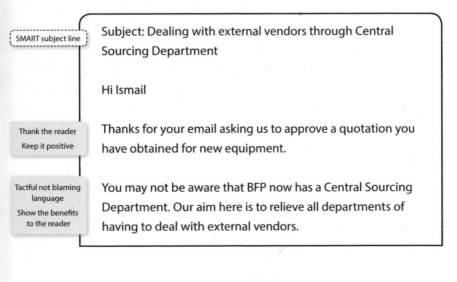

SMART subject line

Subject: Dealing with external vendors through Central Sourcing Department

Hi Ismail

Thank the reader
Keep it positive

Thanks for your email asking us to approve a quotation you have obtained for new equipment.

Tactful not blaming language
Show the benefits to the reader

You may not be aware that BFP now has a Central Sourcing Department. Our aim here is to relieve all departments of having to deal with external vendors.

Obviously in this case you have contacted some vendors already. So I suggest that we work together from here, and of course we will keep you actively involved on the technical side.

Friendly and persuasive

Be helpful, not patronising

With our involvement in helping you with this, and with future projects, our aim is to:

Give reasons why

Bullets are helpful

- Save your time
- Bring potential savings
- Avoid hidden costs

I am attaching our Sourcing Procedures manual, so you can have a better understanding of our role.

Attach relevant documents

Positive close

I'll contact you very soon to arrange a meeting so we can work together on this.

Jonathan

INDEX

ABOUT
THE
AUTHOR

*No matter how much we love technology, we must never
forget the importance of the human touch.*
— Shirley Taylor

SHIRLEY TAYLOR has established herself as a leading authority on modern
business writing and communication skills. She is the author of six successful
books on communication skills, including the international bestseller, *Model
Business Letters, Emails and Other Business Documents*, which is now in its
seventh edition, having sold over half a million copies worldwide.

Originally from the UK, Shirley has lived and worked in Singapore, Bahrain
and Canada. She has over 30 years of experience in teaching and training. After
making Singapore her home in 2002, Shirley established her own company in
2006. STTS Training Pte Ltd has quickly become highly regarded as specialists
in leadership and communication training and speaking.

Shirley conducts her own popular public and in-house workshops on business
writing and email, as well as communication and success skills. Having learnt

a lot from her workshop participants over the years, Shirley has put much of her experience into the pages of this book.

Shirley is also a motivational and success keynote speaker for corporate conferences and events. She puts a lot of passion and energy into her presentations to make sure they are entertaining, practical and informative, as well as a lot of fun.

STTS TRAINING PTE LTD, based in Singapore, is committed to building the competence of individuals and teams to drive performance and results. Our professional, experienced trainers and speakers will engage your teams, and provide them with practical tools and powerful action steps to motivate and inspire them to reach their potential.

STTS is based in Singapore, and we provide services to clients throughout Southeast Asia and beyond.

STTS focuses on four key areas:

- Live Training with popular public workshops and in-house training with professional trainers

- Virtual Training with Shirley Taylor's interactive online virtual training program 'Business Writing That Works'

- Keynotes with inspirational professional speakers

- Online webinars to experience while sitting at your desk

Find out more about STTS at www.sttstraining.com

Find out more about Shirley Taylor at www.shirleytaylor.com

Find out more about Shirley Taylor Virtual Training at www.shirleytaylorvt.com